Travel Ireland

Acknowledgements

Written by Orla O'Brien
Illustration & Design Layout Ailbhe Ryan (ailbhe.ryan@gmail.com)
Creative Director Mark Griffin
Marketing Director Sandra Egan
Publisher Ray MJ Egan
Produced & Published by Page7Media Publishing

With thanks for photographic contribution (including cover images) from: Kevin Morris, Colm Moody (info@moods.
ie), Fáilte Ireland (north, south, east and west regions), Old Irish Images, Ros Kavanagh, An Garda Siochana, Shannon
Tourism, Friction PR, Armagh & Down Tourism, Sean O'Neill and Nigel Clarke.

ISBN 978-0-9554706-0-8

Introduction

opularly known as 'The Emerald Isle', Ireland is a land rich in history – from the legends of prehistory to more recent events such as famine, rebellions, and wars. The country has had a turbulent past and its existence today is testament to the Irish people's resolve to achieve self determination.

In article 4 of the constitution of 1937, the Irish Free State, as it was known, was renamed. 'The name of the state is Éire, or in the English language, Ireland'. This name was derived from Ériu, one of three goddesses, who, according to legend, were the personification of the sovereignty of Ireland.

Our Flag

A tricolour of green, white and orange. The green represents the older Gaelic/Anglo-Norman portion of the country's population, while the orange denotes those of Protestant 'planter' stock, some descendants of supporters of William of Orange. The white signifies the hope for lasting peace between these two communities.

National Anthem

Amhrán na bhFiann (The Soldier's Song) was written in 1907 by Peadar Kearney and Patrick Heeney and officially adopted as the national anthem in 1926.

Irish Government

Ireland is a parliamentary democracy. The national parliament is called the Oireachtas and is made up of two houses: the Dáil (the House of Representatives) and the Seanad (the Senate).

Under Ireland's Constitution, the government must be made up of no fewer than seven and no more than fifteen members. The head of the Government is the Taoiseach (prime minister) who is appointed by the President on the nomination of the Dáil. The Taoiseach nominates one member of the Government to be Tánaiste (deputy prime minister), who will become acting Taoiseach if the Taoiseach should be absent.

The Police

An Garda Síochána (Guardians of Peace) was established in 1922 and is headed by a government-appointed Commissioner. The Gardaí answer to the Minister for Justice, Equality and Law Reform.

National Day

St. Patrick's Day – 17th March
Population: 4,015,676 as of July 2005

People/Culture

The Irish are very outgoing and don't really consider asking personal questions to be offensive. So, be aware that the Irish people you meet will want to know where you are from, how old you are and why you have travelled to Ireland. And, in return for your answers, they will be happy to share (or indeed spin) a few yarns over a couple of pints.

Weather

Ireland has a temperate maritime climate with mild weather conditions in both winter and summer. This mild climate is maintained by the warm North Atlantic Drift and the absorbing effect of the Atlantic Ocean, which soaks up heat in the summer and releases it in the winter.

Coldest months: January and February
Warmest months: July and August
Sunniest months: May and June
Average rainfall throughout the year ranges from 750mm in low-lying zones to 2,000mm in mountainous areas.

Landscape

he island of Ireland stretches 360.30km from North to South and approximately 180km from West to East. It is a relatively small island, which is primarily made up of agrarian country in which bogs cover 15 percent of the landmass.

The country is divided into four provinces: Ulster, Munster, Connacht and Leinster, representing North, South, West and East respectively.

The most northerly point is Inishtrahull Island, which is located just north of the Inishowen Peninsula, at 55.43°N. However, it is worth noting that approximately 400km northwest of Donegal is a small outcrop of rock known as Rockall Island. Ownership is currently being contested between Ireland, Britain and Denmark (which claims it as part of the Faroe Islands) and Iceland. Uninhabited, it is the summit of an extinct vol-

cano and has no source of fresh water – however, ownership of the continental shelf that it lies on will permit that country to exploit its significant resources, such as oil and natural gas.

Ireland's most southerly point is Fastnet Rock, which is located just south of Cork.

The highest peak in Ireland is Corrán Tuathail, which is 1,041m tall and is part of the MacGillicuddy's Reeks range in Co. Kerry.

The island of Ireland is made up of 32 counties. The biggest county is Cork, which covers an area of 7,460km2. The smallest is Louth, covering an area of just 820km2.

The longest river in Ireland is the Shannon, which is 340km in length.

The coastline covers 3,172km, and many Irish beaches hold the prestigious Blue Flag award.

Irish Hillside 7

Irish People

reland is traditionally known as the land of a hundred thousand welcomes (Cead Mile Fáilte), and the warm and friendly Irish people will certainly make your stay memorable. Said to have strong-willed personalities tempered by a quick wit, Irish people are quick to smile in situations both good and bad. One of Ireland's most famous sons, the writer Oscar Wilde, perfectly articulated this optimism when he remarked, "we are all of us in the gutter, but some of us are looking at the stars."

Christianity is the principal religion in Ireland, and it has been a cornerstone of Irish culture since its arrival in 432AD with St. Patrick. Traditionally, Irish people place great importance on family life and the welcome afforded to extended family members has in turn led to the famous hospitality Irish people extend to visitors. An important part of family life is meal times, and Irish people are passionate about their food. Indeed, you'll find yourself spoiled for culinary choice, from traditional favourites such as bacon and cabbage to the ethnic and international cuisine available in some of the finest restaurants in the world.

Ireland has recently experienced a boom in immigration, and the country today is a vibrant multicultural society.

The native Irish language evolved from that of the Celtic settlers, from approximately 600BC. Although Irish survived the Norman and Viking invasions, its use steadily declined, and today it is a first language only in Gaeltacht (Irish-speaking) areas. There are seven Gaeltacht regions in total, and most of them are in the country's most breathtaking yet sparsely populated areas. Four can be found on Ireland's West Coast, in Donegal, Kerry, Mayo and Galway. In the South of Ireland, there are Gaeltacht areas in Cork, Meath and Waterford. Although these regions have made all concessions to modernity, they continue to seek – with Government help – to maintain the Irish language and traditions.

Above: Beach Hurling, Co. Galway, below left: Dame St., below right: Blennerville,Co. Kerry.

Above: High Cross, Monasterboice

A History of Ireland

> *The serious colonisation of the rest of Ireland didn't begin until 1541. Offaly ('the King's county') and Laois ('the Queen's county') were the first counties to be colonised.*

he earliest evidence of human habitation in Ireland dates back to 7000BC, when the first Mesolithic settlers arrived from Britain. The first Celts are thought to have arrived in the country in the early Iron Age, around the 3rd Century BC.

English involvement in Irish history began in earnest in 1159 when Pope Adrian IV granted Henry II the title 'Lord Of Ireland' and encouraged him to invade the country. By 1168, Henry II had been invited by Dermot, King of Leinster, to partake in a joint battle, in which Dermot sought to conquer his rivals and Henry II sought power over the Irish. By the late 1300s, the English had lost much of their hold on Ireland and so Richard

II arrived in the 1390s with the goal of re-establishing control. By the 15th century, the English had created an area of influence known as the Pale, which stretched across Leinster.

The serious colonisation of the rest of Ireland didn't begin until 1541. Offaly ('the King's county') and Laois ('the Queen's county') were the first counties to be colonised. The Desmond Rebellion of 1579 was brutally put down by Elizabeth I, resulting in the confiscation and colonisation of more Irish land. The period from 1607 to 1641 saw the 'Plantation of Ulster' as Protestants from the Scottish lowlands settled in Northern Ireland. Rebellions followed and Oliver

Cromwell arrived in Ireland in 1649 to quell dissent. Cromwell's notorious Irish campaign included the bloody sacking of Drogheda and Wexford. Many of the survivors were sent as slaves to the West Indies.

The Cromwellian settlements of the 1650s resulted in the dispossession of many Catholic landowners and their exile to the sparse, rocky landscape of The West of Ireland (Connacht). Cromwell famously said at the time that the Irish people could go 'To Hell or to Connacht'. Prior to Cromwell's arrival, the proportion of Irish land owned by Catholics was approximately 66 percent; following the Cromwellian settlements, it fell to 10 percent. Forty years on, in 1695, the introduction of the Penal Laws further eroded Roman Catholic power in Ireland.

The late 1700s and early 1800s saw rebellions organised by two of Ireland's most famous patriots. The rebellion of the United Irishmen occurred in 1798 and was led by Wolfe Tone. Founded in 1791, the movement became a secret Republican society, but the rebellion of 1798 was brutally crushed, resulting in the deaths of 30,000 rebels. Another rebellion in 1803, this time led by Robert Emmet, also failed. Emmet was hanged in Dublin, but his speech at his trial became an inspiration for future generations of revolutionaries.

Another important Nationalist figure was Daniel O'Connell, who sought to advance the rights of Catholics through peaceful means. O'Connell became MP for Clare in 1828, and today Dublin's O'Connell Street and is named after him and home to a grand statue in his honour.

By the 1900s, the fight for self determination was nearing an end. The 1916 Easter Rising was an attempted military coup organised by the Irish Republican Brotherhood. The rebellion was intended to occur on a national level, but instead remained confined to Dublin. The Rising came to a head at Dublin's General Post Office (GPO), in which the rebels were besieged by British forces. The leaders of the uprising were captured, and

Eamonn de Valera

The Irish Peace Delegates

Emyvale Garda Station, Co. Monaghan circa 1930.

One of the first Garda Patrol Cars 1938.

Garda Smith on Point Duty 1930.

Poiteen seizure, Co. Mayo, late 1920's.

Michael Collins

Daniel O'Connell (the liberator)

James Connolly (Commandant Genral)

Thomas Clark (Irish Rebellion)

Thomas Ash (Volunteer Leader)

Cathal Brugha

Eamon de Valera

C S Parnell

Padraic Mac Piarais

many were executed. Bullet holes can still be seen in the columns of the GPO and statues in the surrounding area, serving as a reminder of the Rising to successive generations of Irish people.

The Government Of Ireland Act in 1920 specified that the six counties of Northern Ireland would remain within the United Kingdom but granted dominion status to the other 26 counties of Ireland. This situation is referred to as partition. The Irish Free State was founded in the 26 counties with the constitution of 1922; a further constitution followed in 1937, in which the official name of the nation was changed to Eire. This constitution was drawn up under the guidance of then Taoiseach Eamon De Valera, formerly one of 1916 Rising leaders.

Famine sculpture at the IFSC

he Great Famine is one of the most tragic episodes in Irish history. The Famine lasted for four years, from 1845-1849. At that time, the Irish people depended on the potato as their main food source. The famine was caused by a potato blight, which infected the essential potato crops and destroyed them. In the aftermath, cholera, typhus and hunger caused the deaths of approximately 800,000 people.

Workhouses and food depots couldn't cope with the vast numbers of starving people, and soup kitchens were established by some land owners (other, less compassionate, landlords expelled their destitute tenants) and Protestant organizations seeking converts.

The period during and after the Famine saw a mass emigration from Ireland. Altogether, 1 million people emigrated, mainly to the UK, USA and Canada. Since the Great Famine, Ireland has had a special relationship with America, and strong social, political and economic links between the two countries remain today. Approximately 40 million people of Irish descent now live in America.

Irish Myth, Legend & Folklore

reland is a country rich in myth and legend, with many homegrown tales of the supernatural. For generations, Irish people were extremely superstitious, and some superstitions linger in tales still told today. For example, in the past Irish people were very reluctant to tamper with Fairy Raths, stone rings in which these 'little people' were said to dwell. It was considered to be extremely bad luck to build a house on such sites, and it was thought that if people did so, the fairies would trample through their house every night and make life unbearable.

A number of other creatures from folklore continue to be well known today. According to legend, the Banshee is a witch-like woman who howls three times at the bedside of those who have suffered the loss of a loved one. She particularly favours those with the surnames of Flynn, Wynn and Glynn, according to an old rhyme about her passed down through generations. Most people also know the legends about finding a pot of gold coins - said to be hidden by leprechauns, another race of little people – at the end of a rainbow.

Today, such stories seem fantastical, but to many generations of Irish people they served as an important reminder that although the Catholic Church might offer redemption in the next life, there were many happenings in this one, which could not be explained.

Parts of Irish folklore are well over a thousand years old, and these legends are a link between pre-Christian and Christian Ireland. Ireland's myths stretch across three main cycles: The Mythological Cycle, The Cuchulainn Cycle and The Fianna Cycle.

Monks copied the stories of The Mythological Cycle from ancient manuscripts in the 11th and 12th Centuries. Such stories dealt with the Tuath de Danan, which translates as 'the people of Danan', a title which refers to the ancient Goddess Danu. It is said that when the Tuath de Danan were defeated in battle, they went to live underground as fairies. The most famous of the stories from The Mythological Cycle is that of The Children Of Lir.

The story concerns King Lir and his four children, Fionnuala, Conn, Hugh and Fiachra. After the death of his wife, Lir decided to marry again, as he felt his beloved children needed a

Right: The Children of Lir

16

new mother. After much thought, Lir chose Aoife, the sister of his dead wife. Aoife was the most beautiful women in the kingdom and claimed to have virtues similar to those of his gentle wife. How could she not then love his children as his dear wife had?

At first Aoife thrived in her role as queen, but it didn't take long before she grew jealous of Fionnuala, Conn, Hugh and Fiachra, as she realized that the king would never love her as he did his children. Aoife plotted to get rid of the children, and one fine summer's day she offered to take them for a picnic on the shores of their favourite lake. Once at the lake, Aoife began a

magical chant which mesmerised the children. They began to feel piercing pains throughout their bodies and they screamed in anguish as Aoife's spell turned them into swans.

When they had been transformed, Aoife told the children that they were to spend a total of 900 years living as swans. They would live out 300 years on Lake Derravaragh, 300 years on the Sea of Moyle and spend their final 300 years on Inisglora, where they were to stay until Christian bells were heard ringing out across the land. As Aoife was about to leave, she suddenly felt a pang of remorse at her actions, and so chose to leave the four swans with their human voices, so they could speak and sing to one another.

On Aoife's return to the palace, Lir questioned her and discovered what she had done. Furious, Lir grabbed a Druid's wand and pointed it at her, and Aoife disappeared in a puff of thick, black smoke, never to be seen again. Lir immediately rode to the lake to find his children. When he got there, they were much relieved and spoke with their father. Lir continued to visit the children every day, until he made the decision to move his castle to the banks of the lake to be with them. Eventually, Lir passed away but

the children could still bask in the comfort of knowing that they were close to his resting place. When their 300 years on Lake Derravaragh were up, they grudgingly flew north to live on the Sea of Moyle.

The Sea of Moyle was a dark and desolate place, racked by storms, and their time there passed slowly. They were much relieved when their 300 hundred years on the sea finally passed, and they could travel to Inisglora, a beautiful place in which to live out their final days. They began to notice that they were growing old, and their graceful wings were beginning to grow stiff and tired. Eventually, one fine morning the swans heard a strange noise, and realized that it was the ringing of bells. They rushed to the grassy banks of Inisglora, where they were greeted by a monk. The friar was astonished by their story and took them to his monastery. They told him stories of their travels and of older times in Ireland, which the monk carefully recorded in a manuscript.

One day, the monk returned his monastery to find not four beautiful swans, but four ancient people lying huddled together. The Children Of Lir had finally returned to their human forms after 900 years, but their final hour was near. The monk quickly baptized the children and, one by one, they passed away. The monk buried the Children of Lir under an oak tree close to his monastery, where they could finally rest in peace.

They rushed to the grassy banks of Inisglora, where they were greeted by a monk. The friar was astonished by their story and took them to his monastery.

Left: The Fianna Cycle

Illustrations courtesy of Ailbhe Ryan

Religion

atholicism is the principal religion in Ireland, practised by 75 percent of the population. In more recent years, Ireland has seen an increasingly diverse mix of religions, due to a significant influx of foreign nationals, who have been integrated into Irish society.

History Of Catholicism

It is believed that Christianity was introduced to Ireland in the 4th Century from the Roman provinces of Gaul or Britain. The first bishop of Ireland, Palladius, was appointed by Pope Celestine I. His mission was a failure, but he built three churches, the sites of which have been discovered in Co. Wicklow.

By 432AD, a new missionary had arrived in Ireland. St Patrick's goal was to succeed where Palladius had failed and convert the Irish people to Christianity. St Patrick originally came from Britain, from a place in what is now known as Wales. Said to be the son of a Christian Roman official, Patrick was captured by Irish raiders as a boy and brought to Ireland as a slave. Eventually, Patrick escaped and returned to his homeland. However, inspired by a vision that the Irish people were calling on him, Patrick returned

to Ireland to preach Christianity. Famously, St Patrick used the Shamrock (Seamrog), a plant with trifoliate leaves, to illustrate the Catholic doctrine of the Trinity.

Working around the Leinster and Connacht areas, St Patrick spent approximately 30 years on his mission to Ireland. In 444AD, following a visit to Rome, St Patrick founded the cathedral church of Armagh, a city still known as Ireland's ecclesiastical capital today. Currently in Armagh there are two St Patrick's Cathedrals, facing each other on opposite hilltops, one Protestant and one Catholic. The Protestant cathedral was built upon the site of St Patrick's original cathedral and restored around the 19th Century. The neogothic Catholic cathedral was not built until the late 1800s. The grave of the last high king of Ireland, Brian Boru, who died in the Battle of Clontarf in 1014, is located on the site of the original cathedral. A stone tablet marks his grave.

Around the 6th and 7th Centuries, as Europe began to be overrun by pagan 'barbarians', the Irish Church developed a unique method of organisation based on monasticism. Some monasteries grew up around hermits' retreats, but many were established by clan chieftains.

High Cross - Monasterboice
Courtesy of Kevin Morris

23

Family members filled the various monastic offices such as abbott, priest, ascetic or teacher.

According to legend, the Irish monk St Colmcille, whose name translates as 'dove of the church', travelled to Scotland in 536AD in self-imposed exile. It is said that a disagreement with a fellow monk over a copy of a sacred book made by Colmcille eventually led to a great battle, in which many lives were lost. In penance for these fatalities, St Colmcille, also known as St Columba, set off for Iona in Scotland, intending to convert to Christianity the same number of people as had died in the battle.

By the 9th century, monks were commonplace in Ireland, teaching Latin and theology in their schools. Vast libraries existed in Ireland's monasteries, containing countless religious texts. Most monasteries had a Scriptorium in which existing texts were copied or new ones written by monks using pens, ink and coloured pigments to illustrate their books, which were made from vellum or pig's skin. Their techniques are described and demonstrated

The Burren Co.Clare
Courtesy of Kevin Morris

Above: Athenry Castle, Co Galway, below left: Killarney Cathedral, below right: Killkenny Cathedral.

Courtesy of Colin Moody

Above: Quin Abbey, Co. Clare

Courtesy of Colm Moody

for visitors at the Colmcille Heritage Centre in Gartan, Co. Donegal. The Irish monks' manuscripts are some of the finest in history – an example is the beautiful Book of Kells, which is on view at Trinity College in Dublin.

Despite the fact that there were many monastic sites in Ireland, there were very few nunneries. This could be because women had little access to independent funds or land. St Brigid's Church in Kildare is one of very few examples of early Irish nunneries. St Brigid is thought to have lived in the 5th and 6th Centuries and preached the word of God throughout the country. It is said that she preached to a pagan chieftain who was dying, and that she fashioned a cross from the rushes strewn on the floor. The chieftain converted before he died. St. Brigid is commemorated on February 1st , when many people make St Brigid's Crosses and display them in their houses.

It is thought that another nunnery was founded in Clonmacnoise in Offaly. However, it burned down in the early 12th Century, and all that remains today are ruins. Nevertheless, Clonmacnoise continues to be a place of pilgrimage today.

Ireland's most celebrated saint is St Patrick, and the most rigorous of all pilgrimages in Ireland is performed in his name. Taking place on Saint Island and Station Island in Lough Derg, Co. Donegal, St Patrick's Purgatory commemorates St Patrick's visit to the lake at a bleak time for him. The people he tried to convert to Christianity vowed never to believe his teachings until he showed them proof. St Patrick prayed to God for proof and it is said that God showed him a great pit in the ground, which he called Purgatory. The pilgrimage in St Patrick's honour takes place every year (from June to August), during which pilgrims fast and pray for three days. Permitted only one meal a day with black tea or coffee, the barefoot pilgrims spend their time in prayerful reflection.

The people he tried to convert to Christianity vowed never to believe his teachings until he showed them proof. St Patrick prayed to God for proof and it is said that God showed him a great pit in the ground, which he called Purgatory

Architecture

reland is renowned for its architecture, and there are many notable ecclesiastical and secular landmarks throughout the country.

Ecclesiastical Architecture

Ireland's cathedrals have long been popular tourist attractions. St Patrick's Cathedral is located in Dublin's old town. The cathedral is said to be built on a holy well, at which St Patrick baptized converts in the 5th century. Jonathan Swift, one of Ireland's most celebrated authors, is buried in a tomb in St Patrick's cathedral. Swift was the Dean of St Patrick's from 1713-1745.

Ireland's earliest churches were called stone churches and consisted of a single chamber with an eastward facing window and westward facing door. Romanesque architecture was introduced to Ireland from Europe in the 12th Century. Ireland's earliest example of a Romanesque chapel is St Cormac's chapel, situated in Cashel, Co. Tipperary. Gothic architecture, with its unique narrow lancet windows, was brought to Ireland by Continental monastic orders late in the same century. Later religious architectural styles included Planter's Gothic (early 17th Century), Classical (18th and 19th Centuries) and Victorian Gothic (19th Century).

There are a great many church and monastic sites to be seen in Ireland, and a number have been restored for the benefit of visitors. Others lie in ruins, which dot the picturesque Irish landscape. Glendalough, Co. Wicklow, is home to one of Ireland's most important monastic sites. The monastery was built in a valley between two lakes, hence its name, which translates as 'the valley of the two loughs'. It was founded by the 6th Century hermit St Kevin. From this humble beginning, the monastery grew to become an important religious site and centre of learning for the next seven hundred years. It was destroyed in the late 1300s, and the buildings visible today date from the 8th and 12th Centuries. Ironically, Glendalough, once a place of solitude for St Kevin, is now visited by millions of people every year.

Christ Church Cathedral in Dublin's city centre is often cited as Ireland's most exquisite example of ecclesiastical architecture. The cathedral is a combination of Romanesque and early English Gothic styles. In the 11th century there was a wooden church on the site, which was built by Dunan, Dublin's first Bishop. Sitric,

Above: Merrion Square, Dublin,

Above: Newgrange

the Viking King of Dublin, gave the land for the church to Dunan. The Anglo Normans decided to build a stone structure on the site in 1170. Richard De Clare ('Strongbow'), who was The Earl Of Pembroke, instituted the changes. Other important examples of the Norman influence on Irish cathedral architecture are St Mary's in Limerick, St Patrick's in Dublin and St Canice's in Kilkenny. The south aisle of Christ Church Cathedral now serves as a monument to Strongbow. A restoration of the cathedral was carried out by George Street in the 19th Century.

Secular Architecture

Secular architecture in Ireland dates back as far as the Stone Age. Evidence of the country's earliest dwellings has been found at a site in Lough Gur, Co. Limerick, which now houses the Lough Gur Interpretive Centre. Here you can view excavated sites along with an audiovisual film on the life of Stone Age man.

By the Iron Age, Ireland's inhabitants were dwelling in homesteads, ring forts approached by a causeway. Inside the fort, individual dwellings were made from wattle and daub or from stone, with a thatched roof. In the West of Ireland, people lived in stone huts known as 'Clochans', which were built in a beehive shape. You can see these ancient dwellings in Great Skellig, Co. Kerry. Close by is the quaint, Irish-speaking village of Ballinskelligs, with its charming harbour.

Ireland's first castles were built by the Normans, who took great pride in developing Ireland's infrastructure by building towns and markets and establishing trading links. Initially, the castles built by the Normans were those referred to as the Motte and Bailey type. The Motte

Ireland's first castles were built by the Normans, who took great pride in developing Ireland's infrastructure by building towns and markets and establishing trading links

30

Dublin Castle

Above: St.Finbarrs, Co. Cork. Below: Buratty Castle, Co Clare.

Courtesy of Colm Moody

> *Examples of Norman stone castles can be seen at Trim, Co. Meath and Carrickfergus, Co. Antrim.*

was a mound of earth surrounded by a ditch, on which sat a wooden tower. The Bailey section was attached to the Motte and enclosed by a fence. Later, the Normans began to construct much more solid fortifications in stone. Examples of Norman stone castles can be seen at Trim, Co. Meath and Carrick-fergus, Co. Antrim.

Carrickfergus Castle has an interesting history. The castle itself was garrisoned for 750 years up until 1928. This stronghold was the only bastion in Ulster not to fall when the Scottish noble Edmund Bruce attacked. Bruce's siege of the castle lasted for a whole year, from 1315-1316. By the 1700s there were some very strange goings on at Carrickfergus,

Above: The River Liffey. Below: The Customs House.

as Ireland's last witchcraft trial took place here. The year 1778 marked a landmark event for both Carrickfergus Castle and Europe. The first battle involving an American ship in European waters took place in the sea overlooked by the castle. The American pirate captain John Paul Jones in his ship The Ranger attacked a British ship called The Drake.

Around the 13th century, the Anglo-Normans began to make many advances with their architectural technology and added towers and barbicans to their fortifications. However, disaster struck in 1348 when the Black Death, a deadly plague carried by rats, hit Ireland. As a result of the Black Death, the Irish and Norman populations

33

declined to a pitiful level. Ireland went into economic decline, and the Anglo-Normans no longer saw any benefit to investing in Irish infrastructure.

Due to the Black Death, post-1349 secular architecture was built on a much more modest scale. In 1429, the English king Edward VI offered a substantial subsidy to those nobles who constructed castles or towers. A number of towers were built between 1450 and 1650, and the best examples from this period are Bunratty and Blarney Castles. Another castle, built in Thoor Ballylee, Co. Galway, was later converted into a summer house by the poet W.B Yeats.

In 1429, the English king Edward VI offered a substantial subsidy to those nobles who constructed castles or towers.

The 'pirate queen' Grace O' Malley is associated with a number of castles in Ireland. Born into a seafaring family in 1530, Grace soon proved herself to be a worthy sailor and joined her father on the seas. By the age of 16, Grace was married to a chieftain by the name of Donal O' Flaherty, but, despite being married and having several children, she continued to operate as a pirate. Grace is said to have owned many castles across the Mayo area, including Lough Corrib and Rockfleet. In 1584, a noble by the name of Sir Richard Bingham tried to confiscate Grace's castles, so Grace travelled all the way to England to petition Queen Elizabeth I. She was the first Irish woman to be received at the

National Gallery, Millennium wing

English Royal Court, and her castles were duly returned.

In 1804, the construction of Martello towers began, and these defensive towers now dot the Irish coastline near Dublin and Cork, and can also be seen along the Shannon Estuary.

Residential Architecture in Ireland

Examples of thatched cottages can still be seen in many rural areas today. Built from a stone base with a straw thatched roof, the cottage was the most popular dwelling of the peasant classes from the late 1600s. This simple form of architecture was perfectly adapted to the Irish climate. The cottages often had little or no furniture and the number of windows was limited, as more windows meant higher rents. Some of these cottages have been restored and are still lived in today. Visitors can see reconstructions of traditional stone cottages at Bunratty Folk Park and Castle, Co. Clare.

As the country's Anglo-Irish inhabitants became increasingly prosperous in the relatively peaceful period between 1690 and 1798, they began to build well-appointed country houses. In the 17th and 19th Centuries, builders of these houses were influenced by English architecture, but the Italian style of architecture was favoured in the 18th Century.

Above: Dublin City

Above: Adare, Co. Limerick.

The most popular style of house was the Palladian villa. This typically consisted of a central residence flanked by colonnades ending in a pavilion area, which housed kitchens, stables or out buildings. Architect Richard Cassels (1690-1751) introduced Palladian architecture to Ireland in 1728 when he designed Powerscourt House in Co. Wicklow. Other examples of Cassels' work are Newbridge House, Co. Dublin and Westport House, Co. Cork.

In more recent years, Powerscourt House has become a popular attraction for visitors. The estate takes its name from Eustace La Poer, a Norman Knight. Today, the house has been partially restored and there is a restaurant and gift shop on the site. The beautiful gardens, which are on a steep slope facing the Sugar Loaf Mountain, are the perfect place for a leisurely stroll. A few miles from the house is Powerscourt Waterfall. The Dargle River forms the waterfall, which descends 40ft down the craggy rock face. The area around the waterfall includes a children's playground and picnic area and is an ideal spot for families.

One of most important figures in Irish architecture is James Gandon. Lord Portarlington brought Gandon to Ireland in 1781 to design Emo Court Demense in Athy, Co. Kildare. Emo Court is a typical Irish country house, with gardens that are open to the public throughout the year. A guided tour of the house is available from mid June through to September. Gandon's classical architectural style can also be seen in the Four Courts building and The Customs House in Dublin.

A Passion for
Sport

Gaelic football dates back to ancient times. According to legend, whole towns and villages would play Gaelic football games for days on end.

ports on offer in Ireland range from traditional Gaelic football and hurling to such international sports as golf, rugby, soccer, hockey and basketball. The range of sporting facilities in Ireland is phenomenal, and if you wish to catch a game during your stay, there are a number of major sporting venues, including Croke Park and Lansdowne Road in Dublin.

Gaelic Games

The Irish are passionate about the country's traditional games. Most towns and villages have their own Gaelic Athletic Association (GAA) club and grounds. Often, GAA grounds are the central point of a community.

The GAA was founded by Maurice Davin and Michael Cusack in 1884. Both men saw that there was a great desire among the Irish people for a revival of Gaelic games. Davin became the GAA's first president, and its official grounds were named after the association's chief patron, Archbishop Dr T.W Croke. The GAA is now the fastest growing and largest sporting association in Ireland.

Gaelic football dates back to ancient times. According to legend, whole towns and villages would play Gaelic football games for days on end. Gaelic football is played on a pitch approximately 150 yards long and 90 yards wide. All matches are 60 minutes in duration. The aim of this game is to put the football into the opposing team's goal. Players are allowed to carry or dribble the ball. One point is awarded for a ball which goes above the net and between the posts, while a goal garners three points.

Hurling is said to date back to the 8th century. There are two teams in a hurling game, each one made up of 15 players. A hurling stick ('bas'), which is quite similar to a hockey stick but wider, is used to carry and hit the ball. The ball used for this game is called a 'sliotar' and is made from leather and cork. The aim of the game is to get the sliotar across the field and score a goal. A point is awarded for hitting the sliotar between the posts, and three points are awarded for hitting the sliotar into the goal. Camogie is a female version of hurling.

Soccer

The British first introduced soccer, also called football, to Ireland. Originally, it was just played in areas of Ulster, but it gradually spread across

Courtesy of Fáilte Ireland

the country. Indeed, soccer has really only taken off in the Republic of Ireland in the past 20 years. Popularity of the sport in Ireland received a huge boost when the Republic of Ireland team made it to the European Championships in 1988, and went on to beat England in the tournament. Ireland qualified for the World Cup in 1990, when they reached the Quarter Finals, 1994 and 2002. Irish fans travelled in their droves to support their team, and although Ireland has yet to progress further than in 1990, the team has shown great spirit and some promise for the future.

Horse Racing

The Irish are famous for their love of horse racing, and Irish trainers, breeders and jock-

Above: Ballosadare Falls, Co.Sligo

eys are world renowned. Irish horses have won some of the world's principal horse races, and several major race meetings are held annually in Ireland, on world-class racecourses including Leopardstown, Co. Dublin and Punchestown and The Curragh in Co. Kildare.

Fishing

Ireland covers 7,000 miles of riverbank and 3,000 miles of coastline, and this, coupled with the country's climate, lack of pollution and strict regulations, make it a popular destination for anglers. There are three main types of fishing in Ireland: sea fishing, game fishing and coarse fishing.

Sea fishing can be conducted from boats or peers or from the shore, and fish that can be caught in Ireland's waters include cod, eel, mackerel, flounder, mullet, plaice, and whiting. Throughout Ireland, some fishermen offer to take people out on fishing day trips in their boats, and more professional excursions for large groups of experienced sea anglers are also available.

Game fishing is conducted in streams, lakes and rivers. This is a seasonal sport, generally lasting form February through to September. Due to Ireland's huge levels of rainfall, there are numerous inland water areas, offering an abundance of freshwater fish, and trout and salmon are particularly common in lakes and rivers across Ireland. According to experts, light spinning and fly-fishing equipment is best suited to game fishing.

Coarse fishing is an ideal way to take in the beauty of the Irish countryside. The season usu-ally runs form September through to November. Fish caught in this sport include pike, rudd, roach, perch, and bream. Anglers use natural bait, spinners and steel weights when course fishing. Pike caught in Ireland have been known to measure up to 50lb in weight.

Before going fishing, you should contact local fishing associations for recommendations and to find out about license requirements and regulations. Fishing equipment shops can also be a good source of advice. Once you have the correct licence, fishing in much of Ireland is free. However, some clubs own certain waterways, so be sure to find out all the necessary information before your trip. Wherever you go fishing in Ireland, you'll find its one of the best ways to enjoy the Irish landscape, and if you plan your trip well, it's sure to be a memorable experience.

Golf

The Irish landscape is dotted with over 400 golf courses, and golf is perhaps Ireland's major sporting attraction. Golfers of every level are accommodated, and Ireland's golf courses offer innovative designs in beautiful locations. A wide range of course types is available, so you're bound to find your perfect course.

The peak golfing season is from mid May to mid September, and golfers are recommended to book ahead, as these times can be very busy. It's also a good idea to bring along own golf clubs

The peak golfing season is from mid May to mid September, and golfers are recommended to book ahead, as these times can be very busy.

Other Leisure Pursuits

For those who don't have a keen interest in team or highly organised sports, there are plenty of other leisure activities on offer in Ireland.

Hiking And Walking

One of the most active ways to discover Ireland is by hiking or walking across the stunning landscape. There are trails for the most serious hikers and walkers and less difficult routes for those who just wish to take in the scenery. Organised walks take place in various towns and

Ballybunion Golf Course, Co. Kerry

if you have them, as, although many golf clubs rent out equipment, this can also be booked out in peak season. Most clubs also have a strict soft spikes policy, but there's no need to worry if you use hard spikes, as they can be converted for a very small fee.

Golfers travelling to Ireland are in for a unique experience. Some of the best course designers in the world have created Irish golf courses, and the famous Irish hospitality will make your visit a memorable one. In 2006, The Ryder Cup, one of the world's major golfing events, was held on the K Club course in Co. Kildare.

villages across Ireland. There are historic walks led by guides, and often the same routes will be clearly sign posted, so that travellers can go on their own.

Known as the Garden of Ireland, Co. Wicklow offers numerous scenic walks, including one of Ireland's longest walking trails, the Wicklow Way. This walk extends 132km from Dublin to Clonegal in Co. Wicklow and is highly recommended, not just for its great views but also for the many historical sights along the way. Ideal for hill walkers, meanwhile, is the Kilcar Way in county Donegal. This is just one of many scenic or

Lahinch Golf Course, Co. Clare

Far Left: Galway Bay Watch, above: Mirror dinghys in Sligo.

historical walks in Donegal.

Co. Leitrim is another popular destination for walking and hiking. The county offers over 30 different walks, many of them through glacial valleys such as the Glencar Valley. W.B. Yeats' haunting poem 'The Stolen Child' was inspired by the Glencar Waterfall in this area. Further hiking spots worth considering include those in Counties Kerry, Cavan and Offaly.

Horse Riding

Ireland is an extremely popular destination for horse riding, and there are stables in every county in the country. Numerous equine activities are available, including horse riding lessons, polo and pony trekking on the beach. Horses native to Ireland include the Connemara Pony, the Irish Draught Horse and the Irish Cob Horse. Riders of every level are catered for – all riding schools offer tuition by experienced instructors and all horses are extremely well trained.

Cruising On The Irish Waterways

Ireland is home to the Erne-Shannon Waterway, the longest navigable inland waterway in Europe. This route is made up of four sections: The River Erne, The Shannon-Erne link, The South Shannon and The North Shannon. The Shannon-Erne Waterway starts in Belleek, Co. Fermanagh and extends to Killaloe in Co. Clare. No boating licence is required for cruising in Ireland, but it makes sense for novices to arrange some basic tuition beforehand to ensure that they're comfortable at the helm of their boat and that their trip is a safe one.

The main advantage of river cruising is that it allows visitors to take in the sights at their own pace, and, as staying on the boat saves on hotel bills, it is also very economical. For those who would rather not pilot their own boat, plenty of organised boating trips are available.

The main advantage of river cruising is that it allows visitors to take in the sights at their own pace, and, as staying on the boat saves on hotel bills, it is also very economica

Economy

During Ireland's earliest years of independence, the Irish government followed a protectionist policy in which self sufficiency was the key goal. There were a number of barriers to free trade at this time. By the early 1960s, it had become clear that such policies were not working, and as a result successive governments began to make important economic reforms.

uring Ireland's earliest years of independence, the Irish government followed a protectionist policy in which self sufficiency was the key goal. There were a number of barriers to free trade at this time. By the early 1960s, it had become clear that such policies were not working, and as a result successive governments began to make important economic reforms.

Under the leadership of Taoiseach Sean Lemass, Ireland began to refocus its economic policy, placing emphasis on Foreign Direct Investment and the lifting of trade barriers, particularly those which had hindered trade with the USA and Europe. Ireland's entrance into the European Economic Community in 1973 also heralded more prosperous times to come. Nevertheless, the 1980s saw a number of serious economic difficulties for Ireland, including crippling tax rates, high unemployment and mass emigration. Things had improved by the mid-1990s, which saw the beginnings of the current economic boom, dubbed 'The Celtic Tiger'.

By the year 2000, Ireland had become one of the world's fastest growing economies. During the Celtic Tiger period, the Irish economy grew at an impressive rate of 9 percent per annum. As a result of such changes, Irish living standards have risen dramatically and now surpass those of many other western European states.

By 2002, the Irish population had grown to over 4 million, the highest population recorded since the 1870s.

According to Ireland's Department of the Taoiseach, the current goals of the Government are to:

"Build a fair society of equal opportunity and of sustained prosperity on an island at peace with itself" – Mary Harney TD, former Tánaiste.

Ireland, Europe and the Euro

Since 1973 when Ireland joined the European Economic Community, which later became the European Union (EU), the country's relationship with Europe has had important economic implications. One of the most important stepping stones in Ireland's relationship with Europe has been the country's participation in European Monetary Union (EMU).

The new European currency, the euro, was introduced in cashless form on 1 January 1999

Maastricht Treaty

Before the introduction of the euro there was much debate among the 12 Eurozone member states about how each country could retain a sense of national identity with regards to the new currency. A compromise was reached under which the euro coins would carry national symbols and the euro notes would carry European symbols.

when Ireland and the 11 other 'Eurozone' countries permanently set the exchange rates of their national currencies against the euro. Euro notes and coins replaced the 'punt' (Irish pound) as the national currency on the 1st January, 2002.

EMU offered Ireland a number of economic and political benefits. Politically, EMU has meant deeper integration and solidarity among EU member states. However, achieving EMU was not a straightforward process. In order for the 12 Eurozone member states to reap the benefits of monetary union, they had to fulfil the 'convergence criteria' outlined in 1992's Maastricht Treaty.

The Euro

Before the introduction of the euro there was much debate among the 12 Eurozone member states about how each country could retain a sense of national identity with regards to the new currency. A compromise was reached under which the euro coins would carry national symbols and the euro notes would carry European symbols.

Each euro note carries an image of an EU flag along with one of seven designs based on significant architectural periods in Europe's history. Each of the monuments on the notes is a fictional building representing an architectural style – none of the designs show actual European structures.

The windows and gateways on one side of the notes represent Europe's spirit of openness and co-operation, while the bridges on the reverse side represent communication between the people of Europe.

There are 8 euro coins. One side of each coin depicts a generic image of a map of Europe bordered on one side by a line of stars, while the reverse side bears a national symbol of the member state that issued it. Irish euro coins bear the time-honoured Irish symbol of a harp. Although the coins carry different national symbols, every euro coin can be used in every Eurozone member state.

Old Money

Those with an interest in Ireland's pre-euro coinage should head to The Museum Of Decorative Arts in Collins' Barracks, Dublin. The museum is on the route of all hop-on/hop-off tourist buses and is a short walk away from Heuston train station and the Museum Luas stop. Building of the barracks commenced in 1702, and over the years it has housed both English and Irish troops. The Army gave the barracks to the National Museum in 1994.

The museum houses many different collections representing economic, industrial, political and military history in Ireland over the past 300 years.

Entertainment Music and The Arts

Music

usic and performance runs through the veins of the Irish people, and Ireland has produced some exciting musical talents, many of whom have become internationally renowned. Irish music is an eclectic mix that ranges from traditional to classical to modern pop and rock music, so you're bound to find something to suit your tastes.

Traditional Music

Traditional song and dance is an integral part of Irish history and indeed modern culture. Much of the traditional Irish music we know today is known to have originated in the 18th and 19th Centuries. However, some of it is earlier in origin, and it is likely that some very old melodies and lyrics have survived and been adapted to modern forms. Most closely resembling the traditional music of Western Europe, Irish traditional music nonetheless has its own distinctive style, which is sustained by Irish musicians both at home and abroad. It is a form of music learned more by example than by formal teaching, handed down from one generation to the next, or passed from one performer to another. Stu-

dents of traditional music normally learn songs through unconscious or conscious imitation of more experienced performers, although today learning also takes place in organised groups, and occasionally within the formal education system.

One of the most haunting forms of traditional music is sean-nós which, in its broadest definition, is unaccompanied singing in Gaelic. Although sean-nós is no longer widely performed, the tradition has survived and has influenced modern artists such as Sinead O'Connor.

A seisiún (session) is an informal gathering of musicians performing traditional music and song which nowadays mostly takes place in pubs. Seisiúns are usually open to anyone who wants to join in, provided they already know how to play Irish traditional music. Popular instruments used include the bodhran (traditional Irish drum), accordion, fiddle, banjo, uileann pipes (Irish pipes), tin whistle and harmonica.

Traditional Dance

Traditional Irish dancing is still performed widely throughout Ireland today, and has become hugely popular worldwide thanks to Riverdance

One of the most haunting forms of traditional music is sean-nós which, in its broadest definition, is unaccompanied singing in Gaelic. Although sean-nós is no longer widely performed, the tradition has survived and has influenced modern artists such as Sinead O'Connor.

49

Shane McGowan

Ronan Keating

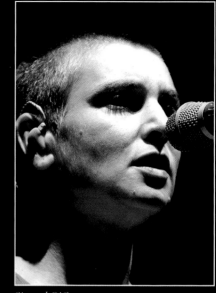

Sinead O'Connor

There is a diverse range of popular music in Ireland, spanning many genres. Radio- and television-friendly pop bands such as Boyzone, Westlife, Samantha Mumba and B*Witched have won the hearts of young music fans worldwide, and continue to be extremely popular.

and Lord of the Dance. Ceilis (traditional Irish dance gatherings) and set dancing can still be found throughout Ireland, and are especially popular at traditional Irish music festivals such as the Fleadh Ceol na hEireann (the National Festival of Irish Traditional Music), which takes place in a different town in Ireland every year.

Classical Music

There is a long tradition of classical music in Ireland and it remains popular today.

One of the most well known orchestras is the RTÉ National Symphony Orchestra which, through performance, broadcast and touring, brings classical music to many parts of Ireland and to the rest of the world. Recent notable performances have included the complete cycles of Prokofiev and Beethoven's symphonies, as well as new work from Irish composers, such as John Buckley, Kevin O'Connell and Benjamin Dwyer.

The National Youth Orchestra of Ireland

The National Youth Orchestra of Ireland was formed in 1970, and is now funded primarily by the Department of Education and Science, its corporate sponsor Toyota Ireland and by the Arts

Council of Ireland. Its members are recruited through a rigorous selection process and, even after their position is secured, they must re-audition annually to ensure the very highest standards are maintained. There are several performing ensembles for various age groups, including the National Youth Symphony Orchestra of Ireland, National Youth Orchestra of Ireland Camerata Strings and the National Youth String Training Orchestra. These ensembles seek to offer their members the best training and performance experience, in addition to promoting the talents of young Irish musicians today.

The Irish Chamber Orchestra

Based in Limerick, The Irish Chamber Orchestra is made up of distinguished Irish string players, and is funded by The Arts Council. This professional ensemble tours regularly both in Ireland and abroad and every year hosts The Shannon International Music Festival, which is considered to be one of the foremost events in the classical music calendar.

As well as past associations with such international stars as violinist Nigel Kennedy and pianist Maria Joao Pires, the Irish Chamber Orchestra commissions homegrown music from Irish com-

Westlife

Above:U2, below: The Frames

Above: Bono, Below: The Thrills

David Kitt

Director

posers, such as Bill Whelan.

The Irish Baroque Orchestra

Established in 1996, The Irish Baroque Orchestra is Ireland's sole professional period-instrument orchestra, featuring some of the most promising young players in the international early music scene, many of whom have worked with the world's finest groups. The instruments they use are either Baroque instruments or modern replicas, and they perform music from the 17th and 18th Centuries in order to give audiences a unique opportunity to hear authentic live performances of Baroque pieces.

Popular Music

There is a diverse range of popular music in Ireland, spanning many genres. Radio- and television-friendly pop bands such as Boyzone, Westlife, Samantha Mumba and B*Witched have won the hearts of young music fans worldwide, and continue to be extremely popular.

Irish talent is also plentiful in the rock arena, from the world-renowned trailblazers U2 to countless up-and-coming musicians, such as Damien Rice, who began his career busking on the street. Many Irish music venues can lay claim to playing a vital part in launching the careers of now well-known musicians. Venues such as Whelan's of Wexford Street in Dublin, Cleere's Bar in Kilkenny and The Spirit Store in Dundalk, Co. Louth, are committed to promoting live music from all genres and offer great entertainment throughout the year.

Famous names in Irish music

Born in 1670, Turlough O'Carolan was a blind, itinerant harpist and composer whose gift for musical composition and poetry brought him great fame. Much of his work still survives today in single-line melody, and he is remembered for his 'planxties' (songs of praise), which he composed for his patrons. His face appeared on the Irish £50 note (pre-Euro currency).

Born in Armagh in 1773, Edward Bunting was one of the most celebrated piano teachers and organists of his time and the first systematic collector of Irish folk songs. In 1792 he was the official recorder at the Belfast Meeting, where he notated the performances of traditional Irish harpists. As a result, he was able to preserve traditional melodies which were otherwise certainly destined for extinction.

Operatic singer and composer Michael William Balfe was born in Dublin in 1808, on Pitt Street, which is off Grafton Street and today bears the singer's name. His musical talents became apparent at an early age and, after performing his first concert at the age of nine, he embarked on a singing career that brought him to England, Italy and France. As a composer, he wrote 28 operas, his most famous being The Bohemian Girl, which was first performed in London in 1843.

The Dubliners are a celebrated Irish folk band who formed in 1962 and still enjoy huge popularity today all over the world. The founding band members were Ronnie Drew, Luke Kelly, Ciaran Bourke, John Sheehan and Barney McKenna. Bourke left the group due to ill health in 1974, and died in 1988. The band continued but tragedy again struck when Kelly was diagnosed with a brain tumour in 1980. He continued to appear with the band until two months before his death in 1984. The band have continued to see many lineup changes throughout the years, but have remained faithful to their traditional style. With McKenna and Sheehan the only remaining original members, The Dubliners continue to play to packed houses today.

The Chieftains are a Grammy-award-winning Irish traditional band, formed in 1962. The band's leader is Paddy Moloney, and he composes and arranges much of the band's music. The band has recorded numerous albums of instrumental traditional Irish folk music, as well as collaborating with popular musicians of many genres, from country to rock and roll.

Born in Newbridge, Co. Kildare, Christy Moore is an internationally renowned traditional musician and singer-songwriter. Once a bank clerk, he formed the acclaimed group Planxty in 1972 with old school friends Andy Irvine, Donal Lunny and Liam O'Flynn. Lunny left in 1974 and Moore followed him in 1975, but the two got together again to form Moving Hearts in 1981. Moore lasted only two years with

Moving Hearts before leaving to forge a highly successful solo career. One of Ireland's best-loved musicians, he published his autobiography in 2000.

Rory Gallagher was an Irish blues and rock guitarist born in 1948 in Ballyshannon, Co. Donegal, but raised in Cork. He first played with showbands, but in 1966 he formed the rock band Taste, who released two excellent studio albums, Taste and On the Boards. The band split in 1970 following an appearance at the Isle of Wight festival and Rory pursued a solo career until his untimely death in 1995, aged just 47. He sold over 30 million albums worldwide but is perhaps best remembered for his incendiary live performances.

Phil Lynott was born in England in 1949 to a Brazilian father, Cecil Parris, and an Irish mother, Philomena Lynott. However, his father and mother split soon after his birth and he was brought up in Dublin by his grandmother Sarah. A songwriter and musician, he formed Thin Lizzy in 1969; the band enjoyed great success and are probably best known for their hit songs Whiskey in the Jar and The Boys are Back in Town. The band broke up in 1983, and Lynott's last years were dogged by drug and alcohol addiction. In December 1985 he had a health breakdown caused by a heroin overdose from which he was never to recover, dying in hospital in January 1986 at the age of just 36. In 2005, a life-size bronze statue was erected in his honour on Dublin's Harry Street, outside Bruxelles pub.

Rory Gallagher

Phil Lynott

U2 are one of the most celebrated rock bands in the world today. Fronted by the charismatic Bono (a.k.a. Paul Hewson), the group – also comprising drummer Larry Mullen, bassist Adam Clayton and guitarist The Edge (a.k.a. Dave Evans) – have sold over 170 million albums worldwide, had six Number One albums in the US and nine Number One albums in the UK. Bono has used his fame to assist those in need, forming strong allegiances with high profile figures such as Nelson Mandela and Tony Blair in an effort to bring attention to the plight of impoverished children in Third World countries. He has worked with groups and charities such as Live Aid, the African Well Fund, DATA (Debt, AIDS, Trade in Africa), the Jubilee Debt Campaign, Live 8 and Make Poverty History. As well as having homes all over the world, the four band members still have residences in Ireland – Bono and The Edge live in Dalkey, Mullen lives in Howth and Clayton in Rathfarnham.

The Pogues, originally known as Pog Mahone (from the Gaelic Póg Mo Thóin,

meaning 'kiss my arse'), were formed in 1982. Their music incorporated genres such as punk rock and Irish traditional, something that was completely new at the time. It was this unique sound, coupled with exciting live performances, rebellious attitudes and their inimitable frontman, Shane MacGowan, that led to the legendary status they hold today. MacGowan embarked on a long hiatus from the Pogues in the 1990s and for a while pursued a solo career with new backing band The Popes. During this period, he also collaborated with many artists, including Christy Moore, The Jesus & Mary Chain, Van Morrison, Nick Cave and Sinead O'Connor. The Pogues reformed in 2001 for an ongoing series of sold-out tours, but they have yet to record any new music.

Born Eithne Ni Bhraonain in 1961 to a musical family in Gweedore, Co. Donegal, Enya is one of the world's leading recording artists. In 1980, she joined Clannad, the band composed of her siblings Máire, Pól, and Ciarán and uncles Noel and Padraig Duggan. She left the group in 1982 to pursue a

solo career, teaming up with former Clannad manager Nicky Ryan, who produces her albums, and his wife Roma, who writes her lyrics in various languages. A Grammy-award-winning artist, Enya attributes her success to the collaboration of all three people involved.

Central to the development of young Irish groups today is Dublin band The Frames. Formed in the early 90s, they are hugely popular in Ireland, the US and Europe, yet despite their success they have continued to help many up-and-coming Irish bands. The name of the band refers to lead singer Glen Hansard's habit of fixing the bicycles of friends and neighbours as a child. As a result, his house was filled with bicycle frames and it became known as 'the house with the frames'.

Singer-songwriter Damien Rice was born in Celbridge, Co. Kildare, in 1970. His music is filled with poetic lyrics and haunting melodies and has launched him onto the international stage. He has enjoyed huge success with his debut album, O.

Damien Rice

Theatre

It was only after the establishment of the Irish Literary Theatre, which would later become known as The Abbey, that homegrown Irish talent could be promoted.

he small island of Ireland has made a significant, and somewhat disproportionate, contribution to English-speaking drama. Although there are documented performances of plays on religious themes in Ireland as early as the 14th century, plays performed in Irish theatre's early days tended to conform to the political purposes of the ruling British administration. However, as more theatres opened and the popular audience grew, a more diverse range of performances became available. A number of Dublin-based theatres developed links with their London equivalents and performers and productions from England often found their way to the Irish stage. However, most Irish playwrights – from Oliver Goldsmith in the 18th Century to George Bernard Shaw in the 20th - found it necessary to go abroad to establish themselves. It was only after the establishment of the Irish Literary Theatre, which would later become known as The Abbey, that homegrown Irish talent could be promoted. Founded in 1903 by William Butler Yeats and Lady Augusta Gregory, the Abbey Theatre alongside An Taidhbhearc (an Irish language theatre founded in 1928) combined to promote the production of plays in both Irish and English, and helped to retain Irish dramatic talent.

Today, theatre in Ireland is just as exciting with productions new and old performed in countless theatres around the country, with the best of Irish and international talent on show.

Famous Irish Writers

Oscar Wilde

...was one of Ireland's best-known playwrights. Born in Dublin in 1854, he studied in Trinity College, Dublin, and later at Magdalen College, Oxford. He lectured to great acclaim in Britain, the United States and Canada and in 1891 produced his only novel, The Picture of Dorian Gray. The book was well received but Wilde's creative flair was perhaps best illustrated in his plays – Lady Windermere's Fan, A Woman of No Importance, An Ideal Husband, and The Importance of Being Earnest, widely regarded as his masterpiece. Although married with children (he married Constance Lloyd in 1884 and they had two sons, Cyril and Vyvyan) Wilde conducted a number of homosexual affairs, the most infamous of which was with Lord Alfred Douglas (nicknamed "Bosie"), son of the Marquess of Queensberry. The

Oscar Wilde

Bram Stoker

Maeve Binchy

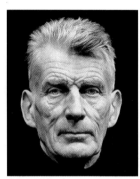

Samuel Beckett

Christy Brown

Marianne Keyes

affair eventually led to Wilde being sentenced to prison for two years for gross indecency. His experiences in jail inspired his most famous poem, The Ballad of Reading Gaol, and in 1905 a letter written to Douglas while Wilde was in jail was published under the title De Profundis. After his release, Wilde was a broken man, and spent his last years in Paris without fame or fortune under the assumed name of Sebastian Melmoth. He died in Paris in 1900 at the age of 46 and is buried in Père Lachaise Cemetery.

Bram Stoker

Abraham "Bram" Stoker was born in Clontarf in Dublin in 1847, and his early years were dogged with illness. However, he recovered fully and later attended Trinity College, graduating with a degree in mathematics. He followed his father's wishes by working as a Civil Servant and, during this time, wrote stories and worked as a theatre critic for Dublin newspaper the Evening Mail. In 1878 he married Florence Balcome with whom he had one child, a son named Noel. The couple moved to London, where Stoker became business manager of the Lyceum Theatre. To supplement his income, he wrote a number of novels, his most famous being the vampire tale Dracula, which he published in 1897. None of his other novels achieved the lasting fame or success of Dracula, which has gone on to inspire countless films, plays and TV shows.

Samuel Beckett

The gifted playwright, novelist and poet Samuel

The Abbey Theatre

Courtesy of Ros Kavanagh

Hysteria

Rattled and Disappeared

Beckett was born in Foxrock, Co. Dublin, in 1906. He studied at Trinity College and, after teaching briefly in Belfast, moved to France to lecture at the Ecole Normale Supérieure in Paris. While in Paris, he was introduced to James Joyce and worked as an assistant to him, most importantly conducting research for that would become Joyce's final novel, Finnegan's Wake.

Beckett's own work was stark, minimalist and concentrated on human suffering and survival. He is perhaps most renowned for the play Waiting for Godot, about which the critic Vivian Mercier wrote that Beckett "has written a play in which nothing happens, twice."

In 1969, Beckett was awarded the Nobel Prize for Literature. His wife Suzanne, whom he had married in 1961 after a 23-year-long companionship, described the award as a "catastrophe," fearing her intensely private

husband would be saddled with fame.

Both Beckett and his wife died in 1989 – Suzanne in July and Samuel in December – and are buried together in Cimetière du Montparnasse in Paris.

Christy Brown

Christy Brown was born in Crumlin, Dublin, in 1932. He suffered from cerebral palsy and was thought to be brain damaged until he began writing and painting with his foot. His autobiography My Left Foot was an international best seller and was translated into 14 languages, as well as being made into a movie by Jim Sheridan. Other Brown works include A Shadow on Summer and a collection of poetry, Come Softly to My Wake. He lived with his wife Mary Carr in Somerset, which is where he died in 1981.

Maeve Binchy

Born in Dublin in 1940, Maeve Binchy is a popular novelist who has penned several romantic novels and short stories that have achieved worldwide success, including Circle of Friends, which was made into a movie. She currently lives in Dublin with her husband, writer and broadcaster Gordon Snell.

Marian Keyes

Born in Limerick in 1963, Marian Keyes was brought up in Dublin. Despite studying law and accountancy at University College Dublin she never seriously pursued that career and moved to London in her 20s, where she began to write short stories. Her first novel, Watermelon, was published in 1995 and became a worldwide success. Her subsequent novels were equally successful, and her work has been translated into 32 languages.

Art
and Sculpture

"

During the 1800s it became fashionable for Irish artists to travel abroad to learn from their peers. Among those to travel to London at this time were Martin Arthur Shee and Daniel Maclise. Other artists travelled to France, including Nathaniel Hone, who was influenced by the Barbizon school, and Roscommon artist Roderic O'Connor. In 1823, The Royal Hibernian Academy was founded to offer many young Irish artists the chance to exhibit their works.

"

arly carvings found at sites such as Newgrange to the ornamental gold objects, religious carvings and illuminated manuscripts of the medieval period, prove Ireland has a strong artistic history. Ireland's modern artistic movement truly began with the foundation of the Dublin Society Schools in 1746. The main focus of the society was the promotion of design in art and industry in Ireland. One of the school's most famous pupils was artist Hugh Douglas Hamilton (1739 -1808), who painted pastel portraits and later studied oil painting in Italy.

18th Century Irish landscape artist Susanna Drury painted magical scenes of the Giant's Causeway in Antrim, which can be viewed in The Ulster Museum.

Around the time Drury was acquiring fame, sculptor and pupil of the Dublin Society Schools Edward Smyth was hard at work. Smyth created the Riverine heads on the keystone arches of Dublin's Custom House. During the construction of the Four Courts, Smyth worked alongside the fine architect James Gandon. Smyth also contributed to the construction of Dublin's Bank Of Ireland building.

The most significant artistic figure of the

1700s was James Barry. Barry painted large-scale neo-classical works, and developed his skills as a painter and sculptor in a number of countries, including Italy.

During the 1800s it became fashionable for Irish artists to travel abroad to learn from their peers. Among those to travel to London at this time were Martin Arthur Shee and Daniel Maclise. Other artists travelled to France, including Nathaniel Hone, who was influenced by the Barbizon school, and Roscommon artist Roderic O'Connor. In 1823, The Royal Hibernian Academy was founded to offer many young Irish artists the chance to exhibit their works.

One of Ireland's most famous sculptors, John Hogan arrived on the scene in the late 1800s. Two of Hogan's contemporaries, Patrick MacDowell and John Henry Foley, travelled to London to work on the Albert Memorial. Foley created the memorial's bronze statue of Albert, and also sculpted three fine works in Dublin: The O'Connell Monument on Dublin's O'Connell Street and the statues of Burke and Goldsmith which flank the entrance to Trinity College, Dublin.

The 20th Century produced many notable

Above: Crann an Óir (Golden Tree) outside Central Bank, below left: Sculpture at Trinity College Dublin, below right: Newgrange, Co. Meath

James Joyce

Sculpture at O'Connell St.

Irish artists, including Paul Henry, William Orpen, Sean Keating, Patrick Tuohy, Mainie Jillett and Evie Hone. However, the greatest Irish artist of this era was probably the painter Jack B. Yeats. Brother of the celebrated poet W.B. Yeats, Jack employed a vigorous painting technique, often applying bright colours in thick layers in his unique depictions of everyday Irish life.

The National Gallery Of Ireland on Clare Street in Dublin contains up to 2,000 works, and is definitely worth a visit. The museum currently houses works by major artists including Jack B. Yeats, Evie Hone, Caravaggio, Metsu and Louis De Brocquy. The gallery puts on special exhibitions throughout the year, so be sure to check their

website, www.nationalgallery.ie, before attending. For those keen on learning more about art, the gallery offers lectures by figures from both the Irish and international art scenes.

Dublin is also home to another world-class art museum: the Hugh Lane Gallery on Parnell Square. The museum houses a unique collection of Irish and European works from the 19th, 20th and 21st centuries. Irish artists whose works are permanently on show include Nathaniel Hone, John Lavery, William Orpen, Roderic O' Connor and Jack B. Yeats. Works by European artists include those by Monet and Corot.

Wolfe Tone

Ireland's Festivals

Numerous festivals take place in Ireland every year. The majority are held in the summer months, although notable events also take place in other seasons. Themes include music, food, theatre, comedy, even matchmaking, so you're bound to find an Irish festival that appeals to you, whatever your tastes.

St Patricks Festival.

St Patrick's Festival is held in honour of Ireland's patron saint and for four days Dublin is transformed with street theatre, live music and fireworks displays to create an unforgettable experience for all. Regional celebrations are held around Ireland and elsewhere around the world, many

counties join in the celebrations. Hwoever, there is nothing quite like the excitement of being at the heart of the even in Dublin.
www.stpatricksday.ie

Cork Jazz Festival

The cork jazz festival runs from October 27th through to the 30th. The festival is one of Ireland's most celebrated and largest festivals, with twenty five countries yielding one thousand musicians taking part in the event. Visitors are entertained in over eighty locations across the city throughout the day and night.
www.corkjazzfestival.com

Belfast Festival At Queens

Since the late sixties, The Belfast Festival has been and still is the largest art and cultural event on Ireland's calendar year. The best in international artists are brought to Belfast and much attention befalls the intriguing city. All art forms are celebrated including theatre, dance, literature, jazz and pop music, comedy and visual arts. Approximately fifty thousand attend the festival, which normally runs from October through to November.
www.belfastfestival.com

St. Patrisck's Day Parade

Courtesy of Fáilte Ireland

Left: St. Patrisck's Day Parade, below top: Festival of World Cultures, below bottom: St. Patrick's Day Parade.

Courtesy of Fáilte Ireland

Festival Of World Cultures.

The festival of world cultures is supported by south Dublin's Dun Laoighre Rathdown local council. It's specialty is presenting music from across the globe and is definitely Irelands most mulit-cultural event. Throughout this festival fifty countries are featured in one hundred and sixty events across forty venues. Approximately two hundred thousand people will attend the event which has been described as "Irelands most family friendly festival".
www.festivalofworldcultures.com

The Rose Of Tralee

The Rose Of Tralee is one of Ireland's oldest and most favoured festivals. Every year beauties from across the globe line up for a chance to secure this prestigious title. The women themselves must be of Irish ancestry or birth in order to partake in the pageant. Importantly the title is awarded based on the Roses character and charm as opposed to beauty alone. The streets of Tralee come alive for the event with concerts and street performers all under special street lighting which culminates in one of the most exciting parties of the year.
www.roseoftralee.ie

Puck Fair

Killorglan the geographical heart of Kerry is home to Puck Fair. Zany it is, but Puck fair is one of Ireland's most ancient festivals. During the fair a rather large Billy Goat from the surrounding area is placed on a throne for three days and nights of antics. Puck fair is held without fail on the 10th, 11th and 12th of August every year and will entertain the whole family.
www.puckfair.ie

Galway International Oyster Festival

The medieval city of Galway hosts one of the longest running festivals in the world and lauded as one of the best. From small beginnings with just thirty four guests in attendance at the first festival in 1954 to the internationally renowned event that it is today. Taking place at the end of September, the festival offers exquisite food and non-stop entertainment from beginning to end.
www.galwayoysterfest.com

County Dublin

Dublin city is one of Europe's most attractive and exciting destinations, renowned for its architecture, people and history. An economically and socially vibrant place, Dublin is Ireland's capital, and its current population stands at approximately one and a half million.

Irelands's Eye

Courtesy of Kevin Moran

Dublin city is one of Europe's most attractive and exciting destinations, renowned for its architecture, people and history. An economically and socially vibrant place, Dublin is Ireland's capital, and its current population stands at approximately one and a half million.

'Eblana' was Dublin's first name according to maps drawn out by Ptolemy, which date back as far as the 2nd century. The oldest evidence of life in Dublin, a pre-Christian burial site, dates back to 4,000 years ago, and is situated in the city's Phoenix Park.

The first major settlement dates back to 841AD when the Vikings settled where the River Liffey meets the River Poddle, an area now known as Wood Quay. The name 'Dublin' derives from the Irish name 'Dubh Linn', meaning black pool and refers to the dark appearance of the River Poddle, which is now a subterranean river flow-ing underneath Dublin Castle. Baile Átha Cliath, the city's Irish name and one which is still used, translates as 'town of the hurdle ford' and refers to the hurdles that were used to cross the River Liffey.

In 1014 Brian Boru, the last High King of Ireland, challenged the Dublin Vikings to a battle in Clontarf in Co. Dublin, where the Norsemen were defeated.

The 12th Century saw the first Norman invasions of Ireland. As a result of the defeat of the Irish in these battles, Dublin was granted to the port of Bristol by King Henry II and became a very important trading post. Although the Irish continued with their attacks and the English hold on the area did weaken at various points, the English presence remained strong and influential for hundreds of years to come. Dublin went on to be the focal point from which the English organised their conquests of other parts of Ireland.

From its medieval origins, Dublin has grown into a modern conurbation. The Dubs' pride themselves on their hospitality and enthusiastic approach to life. Dublin serves as the place of operations for the Irish Government and the residence of the Irish president, Mary McAleese. The official residence of the President of Ireland is known as Áras an Uachtaráin and is situated in the Phoenix Park. Park Ranger Nathaniel Clements built the original house in 1751. In 1782 it was acquired for use by the Viceroys who administered British rule in Ireland. It wasn't until 1938 that it became the official residence of the President of Ireland, and it was occupied by the nation's first president, Douglas

Above: Trinity College Library, below: James Joyce Bridge

Above: Sean O'Casey Bridge, below: Grafton St.

Ha'Penny Bridge Dublin

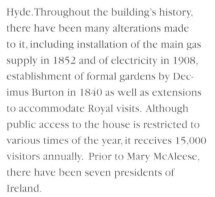

Hyde. Throughout the building's history, there have been many alterations made to it, including installation of the main gas supply in 1852 and of electricity in 1908, establishment of formal gardens by Decimus Burton in 1840 as well as extensions to accommodate Royal visits. Although public access to the house is restricted to various times of the year, it receives 15,000 visitors annually. Prior to Mary McAleese, there have been seven presidents of Ireland.

Dublin's key tourist district is the city centre, which stretches from St. Stephen's Green on the south side across the city to O'Connell Street on the north side, crossing the river Liffey on its way. There are many famous landmarks throughout the city, including the much-loved Molly Malone statue at the bottom of Grafton St., honouring Ireland's famous fishmonger, who tragically died of a fever, and The Spire on O'Connell Street. The Spire is the tallest sculpture in the world and stands on the former site of Nelson's Pillar, which was destroyed by an IRA bomb in 1966. Following the destruction of the statue, a vigorous debate ensued about what to do with the site. This deliberation lasted over 30 years, but it was eventually decided to hold a design competition to find a structure to fill the space, and The Spire design by Ian Ritchie Architects was the winner. The Spire was originally intended to be in place by 2000 to coincide with millennium celebrations, but construction was hampered by delays and the sculpture was finally erected in 2003.

Dublin is also home to the International Fund Services Centre (IFSC). Set up in 1987, it was the brainchild of Dermot Desmond, who says it all began at a meeting in the Shelbourne Hotel in the mid 1980s. He and some other businessmen had been called together to create ideas for revenue generation for the State. Ireland was in a financial depression at the time, and his idea initially met with some resistance, due to a fear of failure. However, this was eventually overcome and with the help of the then Taoiseach, Charles Haughey, the IFSC was established at a site in the Dublin Docklands, and has flourished ever since.

The centre is the hub of the Irish busi-

Above: Moore St. Market, right: Trinity College

ness world, and many Irish and International financial companies have relocated there. In addition to financial institutions, the complex houses hotels, restaurants, and bars, and seasonal cultural festivals are hosted there.

Exploring Dublin's Old Town

Dublin's old town is situated between the Liffey and The River Poddle. Originally a Viking settlement, it was divided into many districts, including the High Street, The Corn Market, The Liberties and Fishamble Street, and most of these are still in existence.

Fishamble Street was selected as the venue for the world premier of Handel's

Above: Custom House and Liberty Hall, below: Mulligans Pub, Poolbeg St, Dublin

'Messiah' on 13th April 1742. An annual festival is now held to celebrate Handel's time in Dublin.

St. Patrick's Cathedral and Christchurch Cathedral can both be found in the old town and are cited by many as Ireland's principal ecclesiastical wonders. Ireland's oldest library, Marsh's Library, is situated beside St. Patrick's Cathedral. Founded by Sir William Robin, it was intended to be Ireland's first public library, and is now made up of four different collections, which comprise over 25,000 books. Most books in the library are still in their original cases. The library's most ancient manuscripts are housed in three purpose-built cages.

Tailors' Hall is situated in close proximity to Christchurch Cathedral. It is the only

Hazy Sunset Skerries

surviving guild hall in Ireland and now houses An Taisce (The Treasury) offices. The United Irishmen, a republican movement led by Wolfe Tone, had many of their meetings here, earning the building the nickname 'Black Lane Parliament'.

Situated across the road from Tailors' Hall is St. Audeon's church and gate. St. Audeon's is the oldest church in Dublin. Its 12th Century tower is the oldest in Ireland and also shelters the oldest church bells in the country, which date back to 1423. The Gate in St. Audeon's is one of the 32 which punctuated the Norman city walls.

Situated on the Liffey, the Brazen Head pub is just a short walk down the road from the Christchurch area in Dublin 8. There has been a tavern on this site since the 12th Century, and the Brazen Head was used as the headquarters of the United Irishmen in the 1790s. The pub is still hugely popular and continues to be frequented by locals and visitors alike. With live music every night and traditional Irish food on offer, an evening at The Brazen Head is a must.

South and North of the Liffey

The St. Stephen's Green area is one of the principal landmarks on the south side of Dublin. At its heart is a park, which is the earliest and largest of Dublin's Squares (others include Merrion Square and Fitzwilliam Square). In the early 18th Century it was the site of public hangings, but it was rescued by Lord Ardilaun (Sir Arthur Edward Guinness, of the black stuff fame!) who funded the rejuvenation, and was responsible for its layout, most of which survives today.

The gate into the park is known as Fusilier's Arch, and is a monument to the many men of the Royal Dublin Fusiliers who lost their lives in the Anglo-Boer war at the end of the 19th Century. It is also known to many as Traitors' Arch, so-called because those Irish soldiers fought on the side of the British against the South African Boers.

During the 1916 Rising, the Irish Citizen Army took up a defensive position in the park, but were overrun by the British Army, which took up a position in the local Shelbourne Hotel, overlooking the park.

Above: Evening on the River Liffey, below right: Bank of Ireland, College Green, Dublin

Today, the park is made up of different gardens, which combine to make a public space with lawns, playgrounds, fountains and flowerbeds. There is also a bandstand, which is still used today. The park provides a welcome respite from the hustle and bustle of town life. Throughout the park there are many monuments, including those in memory of William Butler Yeats, James Joyce, Countess Markievicz, Wolfe Tone and the Great Famine, each serving as reminders to some of Ireland's greatest or saddest times.

On Dawson Street, a road running perpendicular to St. Stephen's Green, is the Mansion House, the official residence of the Lord Mayor of Dublin. It was built in 1710 by property developer Joshua Dawson (whose name is commemorated in the name of the street), who originally lived

Sunset, Skerries, Co.Dublin

in the house. In 1715, the building was purchased by Dublin Corporation to be used as a residence by the Lord Mayor. The price was £3,500, and they also agreed to a yearly rent to Dawson of 40 shillings along with a 6lb loaf of double-refined sugar each Christmas. In return, he would build an extra room in the house, to be used for civic receptions. This was to become the famous Oak Room. Uniquely, this building continues to be a private residence in addition to hosting public functions.

O'Connell Street is the main thoroughfare on the north side of the city. It was developed by the Moores, the Earls of Drogheda, and known then as Drogheda Street. Later it was known as Sackville Street before being renamed again, this time after the great Daniel O'Connell. Known as 'The Liberator', he was leader of the Catholic Emancipation movement of the early 19th Century. A huge statue of O'Connell is located on the street – the four angels at the base represent the four provinces of Ireland: Ulster, Munster, Leinster and Connacht.

Dublin's Writer's Museum is situated at the top of O'Connell Street, in 18 Parnell Square. The building is an original 18th Century house and contains a library, gallery and administration area. It pays homage to Dublin's best literary talents and displays paintings, busts, manuscripts, photos and personal belongings of these internationally renowned writers. Next door at number 19 is The Irish Writers' Centre, which houses the meeting rooms and offices of the Irish Writers' Union, the Society of Irish Playwrights, the Irish Children's Book Trust and the Translators' Association of Ireland. The basement of both buildings accommodates a first-class restaurant called Chapter One - it is haven for literary types and famous for its culinary delights.

The Garden of Remembrance is just across the road from the Writers' Museum. Built by Daithi P. Hanly, it commemorates all those who gave their lives in the name of Irish freedom. At the centre of the garden is a sculpture designed by Oisin Kelly which is based on the theme of the Children of Lir myth, and signifies how people can be transformed by momentous events. The garden was opened by President Eamon de Valera in 1966, on the golden jubilee of the 1916 Rising.

Located on Inns Quay, Dublin 8, The Four Courts building was constructed in 1802 by James Gandon, one of Dublin's

Above: The Millenium Bridge, below: The Custom House, right: Crown Alley, Temple Bar.

Courtesy of Failte Ireland

most famous architects. It is considered to be one of the finest examples of neoclassical architecture in Dublin. Originally, architect Thomas Cooley was hired to design the structure, but when he died in 1784, Gandon took over, although he included some of Cooley's original ideas in his own design.

Today, the building houses the Irish High and Supreme Courts. The imposing entrance doors lead into the great Round Hall and the original Four Courts of Chancery,

Exchequer, King's Bench and Common Pleas. Today, however, they are simply referred to as Courts 1, 2, 3 and 4.

The Abbey Theatre is situated on Lower Abbey Street, Dublin 1. Formerly known as The Irish National Theatre, it was founded by William Butler Yeats and Lady August Gregory in 1904. The playhouse on the current site was officially opened as The Abbey Theatre in 1966. As well as presenting modern Irish and European plays, the theatre remains true to its heritage by stag-

ing many revivals of classics from the Irish dramatic repertoire. The building houses a second theatre, known as the Peacock. The Abbey Theatre also offers educational programmes and publications, and it is well regarded as the starting point from which many famous Irish actors launched their careers.

The Chester Beatty Library is situated in the grounds of Dublin Castle and contains collections of both Asian and international literary and artistic works.

Sir Alfred Chester Beatty, born in New York in 1875, travelled extensively throughout his life, and during those travels he amassed an extensive collection, including a huge number of manuscripts and paintings. When he arrived in Dublin in 1950, his private collection was housed in Shrewsbury Road. It was added to and eventually opened to the public in 1957. Beatty died in 1968 and was given a state funeral, the only private citizen to be afforded that honour. An agreement was reached with the Government that the library would remain in trust for the benefit of the public. It was eventually moved to its current site in the grounds of Dublin Castle, where a purpose-built museum building was erected. The current collection includes 270 copies of the holy Koran, Ethiopian and Syrian biblical texts and European manuscripts from the Middle Ages. This library is well worth a visit, which can be arranged by appointment.

Kilmainham Gaol in Dublin 8 is one of the largest unused jails in Europe. Built in 1796, it was a prison throughout Ireland's long struggle for independence, and many of the country's greatest historical figures were interned there. Some of these prisoners lost their lives for offences committed against the Crown.

It closed as a prison in 1924, and was later opened to the public as a national monument. The museum houses a comprehensive collection of documents on the Irish War of Independence, and tours of

Dublin City by night

the gaol visit the chapel, execution rooms and the courtyard where the leaders of the 1916 Rising lost their lives.

Movie buffs may notice that scenes from the films In The Name of The Father and Michael Collins were shot here.

A Day Trip to the Suburbs

For those with green fingers, The Botanic Gardens are a treat. Ireland's National Botanic Gardens were built in 1797 and are situated in Glasnevin, on the north side of Dublin. Covering 19.5 hectares of land, the site of the Botanic Gardens includes glasshouses designed by Richard Turner. In all, there are 20,000 different types of plant species to be found here. One of the most attractive features of the gardens is a walk which starts in the Rose Garden and ends in the Arboretum. The gardens also include a vegetable garden, wall plants, a rockery and extensive shrub beds.

The gardens are easily accessed and open all year round.

Malahide Castle and Demesne is set on 250 acres of land, and located in north Co. Dublin in the picturesque village of Malahide. Interestingly, the castle was owned by one family, the Talbots, for nearly 800 years. Richard Talbot, a knight who came to Ireland with Henry II, was granted the land in Malahide in 1185, and apart from a brief period from 1649 to 1660, when Oliver Cromwell sought to exert control in Ireland, the castle remained in the hands of the Talbot family until 1976. The castle has a rich history, some of which is tainted by tragedy, and it is claimed that many ghosts still roam the building today.

The castle boasts some fine period furniture and is decorated with beautiful paintings throughout. In the Demesne, you'll find the Talbot Botanic Gardens, which boast a fine collection of Australa-sian and Chilean plants, and the excellent model railway exhibition, featuring hand-made models of Irish Trains. Open all year round, Malahide Castle is an ideal family attraction.

Howth is a small fishing village, also in north Co. Dublin. The village's streets are scattered with pubs, restaurants and cafés, making it an ideal place for a day trip. The world famous fish shop Wrights is situated in Howth village, and visitors can sample some of Ireland's best smoked salmon here. Howth Head is a big hill ideal for both casual walkers or hikers. If you are able to make it to the top, you'll be rewarded with some breathtaking views of Dublin city. The view encompasses the whole of Dublin Bay, set against the picturesque backdrop of the Dublin Mountains.

Bray Head, another hiking venue, is in the old-fashioned seaside resort of Bray in Co. Wicklow. Bray is easily accessible from

Howth, above: Sunset

Dublin city by Dart, the light rail system which runs along the Dublin coast. The town, which offers pebbly beaches, amusements and ice cream stands, is a popular destination for Dubliners and visitors alike.

Although Dublin is hardly renowned for skiing or snowboarding, the sports are available on a dry slope, considered to be amongst the best in Europe, in the village of Kilternan in the Dublin Mountains. It is available to use all year round, and there are qualified instructors on hand at all times. The resort is easily accessed from all areas of the city, and definitely worth a visit.

Mary Gibbons Tours arrange limited-capacity, personalised tours to places of interest outside Dublin. Destinations include Glendalough and Powerscourt – both of which are located in the picturesque county of Wicklow (known as 'The Garden of Ireland') – as well as Newgrange, the Boyne Valley, the Hill of Tara and the Hill of Slane. Each tour consists of a detailed commentary during the visits to historical monuments and sites. The tours departs from different locations in Dublin city and usually last from four to six hours. Advance booking is required.

Left: Lighthouse, Howth

83

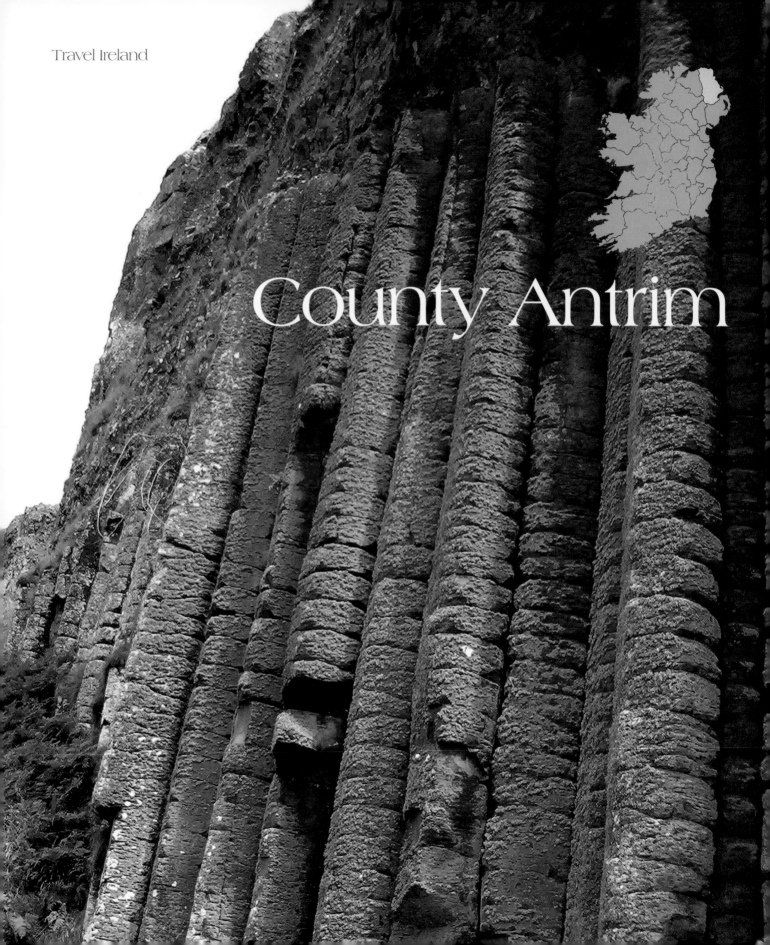

County Antrim

Courtesy of Kevin Morris

Antrim is situated at the northeast corner of Ireland and located on the riverbed of The Six Mile Water, which is close to Lough Neagh.

Originally Antrim was a linen-spinning village and although this still continues extensively today, it is much more than just that.

The Antrim Coastline makes for a great scenic drive. Tiny villages are spread out across the coastline and make for enjoyable stopping points if you should choose to drive the journey. One recommended route is to start in a place called Ballycastle and drive across Antrim to Larne. Across the journey visitors experience a number of Irish wonders such as Ballygally Castle, Carnlough, Cushedon and Glenariff Forest Park. There is also Raitlin Island, which can be easily accessed by boat from Ballycastle. St Colmcille was a heartbeat away from death on one of his journeys in this area when his boat got caught in a whirlpool.

Antrim's most celebrated attraction is The Giant's Causeway. The Giant's Causeway has much history based around Irish folklore. The structures formation is so unusual that many have said that there is no way its origins could possibly be associated with the natural. Many believe that it was the Irish giant Fionn Mac Cumhaill who built the structure in order to travel across the sea the meet a Scottish giant in battle. Those of a more scientific background believe that the Causeway was built as a result of volcanic eruptions, which happened 60 million years ago. At the Causeway there is a heritage centre visited by thousands of tourists every year.

Other areas of interest in Antrim and the surrounding Glens are:

Antrim Castle – dating back to the 12th century this imposing building sits just north of the Glenarm River in the village of the same name. The surrounding land is one of great natural beauty and shouldn't be missed. The castle is also open to the public at certain times, as well as being available to rent - fully staffed!

Lough Neagh at approximately 30km long and 15km wide is the largest freshwater lake in Ireland and the third largest in Western Europe. Irish legend tells that the lake was formed when Fionn Mac Cumhaill took a piece of land to throw at a rival in Scotland – he missed and this piece of land was established as what is known as the Isle of Man.

The lake is renowned for it's eel fishing which is exported to restaurants worldwide.

Pogues Entry Historical Cottage – this was the childhood home of Alexander Irvine, Irish born author, who was a soldier before he left for New York where he graduated from Yale University and went on to preach at the Church of Ascension, 5th Avenue. His book My Lady of The Chimney Corner recounts his time in Pogues Entry.

Left: The Giants Causeway, above: Horses, Co. Antrim

85

Counties Armagh & Down

Armagh is the smallest of the six counties that makes up the North of Ireland, it is known as the ecclesiastical centre of Ireland. It is the one of few cities in the world to have two cathedrals – St Patrick's (Roman Catholic) and St Patrick's (Church of Ireland). The graveyard of High King of Ireland, Brian Boru who defended the country against the Norsemen, can be found in the Church of Ireland graveyard. The cathedral library holds many rare books including and manuscripts including those from Jonathan Swift's Gulliver's Travels. Historical and archaeological collections can be found in The Armagh County Museum as well as modern art collections.

The town of Milford in Armagh was famed for it's linen, but also it is the birthplace of William McCrum who invented the penalty kick. He proposed this rule to stop defenders intentionally fouling the opposing player in order to stop the goal – the rule officially came into being in 1891.

The Market Place Theatre in the centre of Armagh city presents some of the best drama and musical performances around. If you prefer to taste the more traditional Ireland you can enjoy traditional music in the warm and friendly atmosphere of the pubs and restaurants in this county.

St. Patricks Cathedral, Armagh
Courtesy of Armagh and Down Tourism

County Down is home to the Mourne Mountains, which rise to a height of over 2,000 feet and offer the perfect location for walks and treks, with outstanding views of the surrounding landscape. Patrick Brontë, father of the famous novelists the Brontë sisters, was from the Bann Valley – which is now known as The Brontë Country. It is said that the Brontë sisters were inspired by stories of this area told by their father. The school and church at which Patrick Brontë taught and preached have been preserved, and visitors can learn more at the Brontë Homeland Interpretative Centre.

The Ards Peninsula is found between the sea and Strangford Lough, a large sea inlet which is almost completely land-locked. The lough is rich in bird and marine life, making it ideal for bird watching and diving.

Situated on the northern end of Strangford Lough is Newtownards, a great shopping town that also holds a traditional open-air market every Saturday.

At the top of the Ards Peninsula is the seaside resort of Bangor, which has many attractions to entertain the family including yachting, angling and the famous Pickie Family Fun Park.

County Down has been the source of inspiration for some well-known songs, including Percy French's The Mountains of Mourne and Van Morrison's Coney Island, which sees him 'stopping off at Ardlgass for a couple of jars of mussels … in case we get famished'.

87

Counties Cavan, Monaghan & Louth

Field of Rapeseed, Co. Louth

Geographically, Cavan is a link between the North, South, East and West of Ireland. The landscape is often referred to as 'basket of eggs' due to the prevalence of drumlins (rocky deposits left behind when the ice melted at the end of the last Ice Age). Commonly referred to as the Lake Country due to its many streams, lakes and rivers (the source of the River Shannon, the longest river in Ireland, can be found near the Cuilcagh Mountains in the county), Cavan offers many water-based activities such as cruising, fishing and swimming.

Crafts are an important part of Cavan's history. The county is famous for crystal glass making, and the Cavan Crystal Showroom was established in 1969. Here you can select something from their world-renowned range of crystal glass, or from their new range of crafts, including tableware, furniture and jewellery.

Located in the town of Mountnugent, The Carraig Craft Visitor Centre is a basketry museum at which you can see the traditional craft of basket making using rod, rush and straw. In addition to the demonstrations, there are lectures and an audiovisual presentation.

Bellamonth House in the town of Cootehill is a fine example of Palladian architecture in Ireland and well worth a visit. Although the house is private, the grounds are open to the public. Romantically, the town's unusual name commemorates the marriage of Thomas Coote, a colonel in the British army, and Francis Hill. From Cootehill you can visit the Tanagh Outdoor Education Centre, just across the county border in Monaghan, which offers activities including canoeing, banana boating, gorge walking, abseiling, archery and hill walking.

Monaghan is famous as the home county of Patrick Kavanagh, whose poetry was greatly influenced by its landscape. The Patrick Kavanagh Rural and Literary Resource Centre in Iniskeen is

Cabra Castle, Co. Cavan

Castle Leslie, Glaslough, Co Monaghan

a commemoration of his life and work, and a Patrick Kavanagh weekend is held every November, attracting Kavanagh enthusiasts from around the world.

The award-winning Monaghan County Museum, located in Monaghan town's old market house, has displays on the county's medieval past, including some fine coins and artefacts. It also houses the famous Cross of Clogher, a wooden cross with bronze panels thought to have belonged to a saint.

Located in the north of the county, Castle Leslie is home to an equestrian centre, cookery school and hunting lodge and is set in a beautiful area of rolling hills, forests and lakes. It is open to the public for tours of the house during the summer months. The castle is still owned by the Leslie family, who originate in Scotland and can trace their ancestry back to Attila the Hun.

Louth, situated in the north east of Ireland, is the smallest county in the country. It is a fertile land with sleepy fishing villages and busy

towns such as Drogheda and Dundalk, where most of the population reside.

Lying on the River Boyne, Drogheda is one of Ireland's oldest towns and is famous as the location of a gruesome artefact – visitors can view the preserved head of Catholic martyr and saint, Oliver Plunkett, in St. Peters' church. He was sentenced to a brutal death on conviction of high treason, following a very questionable trial.

Carlingford is located in the north of the county, and lies between Carlingford Lough and Slieve Foy. Lying in the Cooley Peninsula, it is linked in mythology to legendary Irish warrior Fionn MacCumhaill, who is said to have roamed this land. Today, the lough is renowned for its oyster industry, and is a wonderful place to stay with a range of activities and entertainments, including water sports, fine dining and traditional music.

Located on the Louth coast 12km from Drogheda is the fishing village of Clogherhead, which boasts the fine Port Oriel harbour, built in 1885. Clogherhead Peninsula is a Natural Heritage area, and is well worth a visit.

Above: Carlingford Lough, Co.Louth, below: Ring Ford Moneygashel, Cuilcagh Mountains, Cavan

Courtesy of Failte Ireland

County Clare

Located on the west of Ireland, Clare is a county of immense scenic beauty. The landscape features the famous Cliffs of Moher which are of the highest sea cliffs in Europe. To the north of the county is the expansive limestone region known as The Burren - here you can find many examples of rare flora, as well as megalithic tombs and Celtic crosses. The Ailwee Caves, the most ancient cave in Ireland, are also located in this area. They were formed by the melt waters of a prehistoric ice age, which carved out an underground channel through the weaker elements of the

Left: The Burren, above: Lahinch Beach, Below: Doonagore Castle, Co. Clare

Doonagore Castle, Clare

Courtesy of Kevin Morris

Cliffs of Moher, Co.Clare Courtesy of Fáilte Ireland

County Clare also features one of the most famous cliff faces in the world. Visited by over one million people annually the Cliffs of Moher tower 250m above the majestic Atlantic Ocean.

limestone land. Features of the cave are stalactites and stalagmites and although many were formed quite recently in relation to the history of the cave, there are some samples of calcite which began to form 350,000 years ago.

Situated as it is, in a Gaeltacht region, Irish is still spoken by many as a first language.

Shannon Airport is located in county Clare and the idea way to visit the west of Ireland.

Courtesy of Fáilte Ireland

County Cork

Cork is Ireland's largest county, and Cork city is its third largest urban centre after Dublin and Belfast. The city centre in Cork was originally built on marshland – often referred to as The Great Marsh of Munster – and the first recorded settlement in the area is that of St. Finbarr in the 7th Century. Cork is a port city and its motto is 'Bene Fida Carinis', which translates as 'a safe harbour for ships'. This attribute has been at the heart of the city's success as a trading centre, but the harbour has also been the scene of great sadness, as it was the main point of emigration after The Great Famine.

Cork city is rich in history. The city was caught up in William Cromwell's campaign in Ireland in the mid 1600s, and it was captured by the forces of William III after a traumatic siege in 1690. In the 1700s many Huguenots arrived in Cork after fleeing from France. This French presence is evidenced today by the city's many French street names. In the early 20th Century, many of the battles in Ireland's War of Independence were fought in and around Cork.

The city also has a long and interesting culinary history. In the 1700s, Cork was the largest butter supplier and had the largest butter market in the world. Cork is also known as a major brewing centre. Beamish and Crawford is the oldest brewery in the city, and Cork is also home to the Murphy's Brewery, which brews a popular stout. The company's name is one of the most common surnames in Ireland – 'Murphy' derives from the Irish word 'Murchadh', meaning Sea Warrior.

Cork has always been a thriving industrial centre. In 1917, Ford set up its first international factory in Co. Cork. Henry Ford had a very strong connection to Cork, as his grandfather was born there and emigrated from Cobh. The Ford factory was shut down in the 1980s, and today most of the industry in Co. Cork is based on computer manufacture.

Cork's city centre is home to many popular attractions. The Crawford Art Gallery holds some of Cork's best art collections, including works by Orpen and Keating. Other exhibits include Japanese Samurai armour and casts from the Vatican. Cork Public Museum house exhibits relating to life in Cork since pre-historic times. One of the most striking examples of ecclesiastical architecture in Ireland, St. Finbarr's Cathedral was designed by the architect William Burges in the French Gothic style between 1867 and 1879.

Situated on Convent Avenue, Cork City

Left: West Cork Fastnet Lighthouse, right: West Cork, Mizen Head, below right: St. Finbars Cathedral, Cork City

Gaol was designed by Sir Thomas Deane in 1825. The prison housed both men and women, and now contains exhibits on the prison diet and regime, as well as displays providing an insight into the types of crimes committed by those incarcerated in the prison.

Cork's beautiful harbour is the second largest in the world, after Sydney Harbour. There are three islands – Fota Island, Little Island and Great Island – in Cork Harbour, joined together by bridges. Situated on

Fota Island, Fota Wildlife Park is Ireland's only man-made wildlife park, and visitors can see the animals from Africa and other continents wandering freely across the park's open spaces.

A number of excursions depart from Cork city, and three worth considering are those to Riverstown House, Dunkathel House and The Royal Gunpowder Mills.

Further afield, the Co. Cork towns of Clonakillty, Cobh, Kinsale Youghal, and Bantry Bay are all worth a visit.

Clonakilty is a National Heritage Town peppered with tall spires, elegant squares and attractive historical buildings. The town was once a thriving industrial centre, but Clonakilty's principal industry today is tourism. Visitors should try the town's local delicacy, Clonakilty Black Pudding. Other attractions include the nightlife (featuring live music, both traditional and contemporary), water sports, horse riding and public gardens.

Historically, Cobh was often referred to as Ireland's gateway to America. Approximately 2 million people left Ireland through Cobh around the time of the famine. The town now commemorates this sad history in its impressive interpre-

Courtesy of Failte Ireland

tive centre, which is open to the public and highly recommended. Cobh is also famous as the port at which the Titanic made its last stop before its fateful voyage to America.

The Anglo Normans founded the small fishing town of Kinsale in 1177. In 1601, the English defeated a coalition of Irish and Spanish troops here, resulting in the 'Flight of the Earls' in which many Irish nobles, including the O'Neills and the O'Donnells, fled their homeland for the Continent. Famous for its restaurants, Kinsale is an idyllic place for hiking, walking, fishing, horse riding, golfing and water sports.

Youghal has a rich history, and artefacts dating back as far as 8,000 years ago have been found there. The Celts are thought to have arrived in the area around 500BC. After the battle of Clontarf in 1014, Youghal became an international trading centre. Much of Youghal's surviving architecture is medieval, and today the town is rich in tourist attractions, restaurants and shops.

The Co. Cork fishing town of Bantry Bay has remained virtually untouched since the 19th Century, and the harbour area of Glengariff has been a popular holiday destination for many years now. Bantry Bay is most famous as the site of a disastrous attempt to land troops during Wolfe Tone's rising – the soldiers couldn't reach the shore and had to return to France.

Courtesy of Failte Ireland

Meath & Westmeath

Meath is primarily an agricultural county and is considered to be one of the most fertile areas in Ireland. The name Meath comes from the Irish 'An Mhí', which means 'the middle'. It is often referred to as the Royal County because the Kings of Ireland resided here on the Hill of Tara. The many castles and ruins to be found in this area are testaments to its former glory.

Meath's principal archaeological site is that of the megalithic structures at Newgrange in the Boyne Valley. Thought to be an ancient burial site, the structures are decorated with a wealth of megalithic carvings, and the meanings of these symbols continue to be debated by experts today. Steeped in legend, The Newgrange structures are estimated to be approximately 5,000 years old, which makes them older than the Egyptian pyramids.

The main river in county Meath is the River Boyne, which is famous as the site of The Battle of the Boyne, which occurred in 1690. The bloody confrontation saw 1,500 soldiers lose their lives in a clash between William of Orange (later King William III) and his father-in-law, King James II.

Located in Ratoath, Co. Meath, Fairyhouse Racecourse is one of the finest in Ireland, and has been home to the Irish Grand National since 1870.

The town of Kells lies to the north of the county, and has historical links with St. Colmcille and the famous Book of Kells, which is now on display in Trinity College university, Dublin.

An inland county, Westmeath is a fertile land peppered with lakes and rivers. Old world charm and modern shopping areas sit side by side in this fascinating county, which also offers the best in leisure activities, including fishing, golfing, boating, walking, cycling and horse racing. Places of interest include the impressive Belvedere House and Gardens in Kilbeggan and the ancient monasteries of Clonmacnoise in Moate, where the breathtaking scenery is the perfect backdrop for a leisurely walk. And regardless of where you are in the county, you are never far away from a welcoming pub or restaurant in which to take a well-deserved rest.

Above and right: Newgrange, Co. Meath, below: Athlone city

Counties Derry & Donegal

Grianan Ailigh Donegal,

Derry is found in the North of Ireland, and is part of the province of Ulster. Often known as the Maiden City due to the fact that its walls were never penetrated during the late

17th Century siege.

Its name is often disputed and is a sensitive issue between Nationalists and Unionists. On the city's Royal Charter it is listed as Londonderry but the name was changed in 1613 to Derry. It is one of the longest inhabited cities in Ireland with the earliest references dating back to the 6th Century.

Amelia Earhart brought fame to the county when she landed there in 1932 - she was the first female to cross the Atlantic on a solo flight.

Across the River Foyle is the Foyle Bridge which is the second longest bridge in Ireland. During poor weather this bridge is closed to traffic. There is a festival held here annually called the Banks of the River Foyle Halloween Carnival where the streets come alive with activities and events for all the family to enjoy.

Golf At Rosapenna Co Donegal

Donegal lies at the far northwest tip of Ireland, the name is derived from Dun na nGall – which means fort of the foreigner and comes from the many Viking raids that were warded off during the 8th and 9th Centuries.

It is the third largest county in Ireland with the least population and is the largest Gaeltacht (Irish speaking) region in the country.

Donegal is renowned for it's rugged beauty, with a lengthy coastline that features many blue flag beaches. Although the weather in this area can be harsh, there are some pockets that are sheltered from the Atlantic.

Malin Head, Ireland's most northerly point is a spectacularly beautiful area and is a popular area for walking, fishing, swimming and photography. Often referred to as 'Ireland's Crown' it is situated on the Inishowen Peninsula and is a haven for bird watching enthusiasts with many rare species to be seen.

The town of Gweedore (Ghaoth Dobhair) is over looked by Mount Errigal which is the tallest mountain in Donegal. From Gweedore you can take ferries to some of the islands that surround Donegal. It is a town famed for its traditional pubs and music, with musicians such as Clannad and Enya coming from the area. There is a strong tradition of sport in the area too with soccer and Gaelic Football being most popular.

Red Deer At Glenveagh

County Galway

Galway has a unique history, which emblazons literary and industrious facets. Founded in the 12th Century, the originally Anglo-Norman city is situated at the mouth of the Corrib River, which made it a huge attraction for trading merchants. Historically it was often referred to as the City of Tribes and was a primary port city forging rich trading relationships with France, Spain and the West Indies. It was with such trading that prosperous families became prominent and thus evolved the name City Of the Tribes. Those fourteen families were Athy, Blake, Bodkin, Browne, D'Arcy, Deane, Ffont, Ffrench, Joyce, Kirwan, Lynch, Martin, Morris and Skerrett and although today Galway is a buzzing cosmopolitan city which has seen many changes,

Storm in Spideal, Co. Galway

many of these names are still evident in the street and business names.

The Spanish Arch is one of Galway's most celebrated attractions. The Arch dates back to when Ireland had trading links with the continent and is situated along Galway's Eyre walk. Eyre Square is definitely going to become party central for those after the nightlife. Day excursions organised from Galway city venture to the areas of Augher-more Castle, Lough Corrib and Oughterard.

Adjoining Galway city are Ireland's most famous Gaelic speaking communities The Aran Islands and Connemara.

There are three different Islands in The Aran group. Inisheer, The smallest, Inish-maan, the middle Island and Inishmoor the biggest Island. The Islands are a haven for Irish fishermen and are steeped in the fishing traditions of Ireland. Over 400 plant

Above: Roundstone, Connemara, below: Derryclare Lough and Pine Island, Connemara

Above: Cliffs at Dun Aongas Below: Quiet Man Bridge Maam Cross, Connemara

species can be found across the Islands. You will notice on your stay there are very few trees, the fields on the Island are very sparse but are separated by really picturesque dry, stone walls which actually add to the allure of the islands. The houses, which are trademark to the Island, are white stone- washed thatched cottages.

The Aran Islands are most famed for their fashion and literary heritage. Aran knitwear, which is cream in colour and made up of a special stitch type, has been worn by sailors form the Aran Islands for years. Stories from the Islands have influenced many of the world's best playwrights from JM Synge's Playboy of The Western World to the film Man Of Aran.

Connemara is reminiscent of Americas Wild West, with barren landscapes, mountains lakes, bog, beaches and unspoilt scenery it is an idyllic place. In recent years areas in Connemara such as Clifden have become the holiday destination of choice for the Irish people and visitors alike, it is not uncommon to find many people having holiday homes in this area. Among the attractions in Connemara are Kylemore Abbey, Clifden Bay, Lough Corrib and Leenane Wool Museum.

Athenry located just outside of Galway city, is a wonderful example of a medieval city complete with castle, church, medieval street plan and medieval town walls. With art and heritage in great supply this is a town worth visiting.

County Kerry

Left: Killarney lakes, above: tour bus, right: Muckross House

Courtesy of Celtic Marvels

Kerry is a very special location. Situated at the most southern tip of Ireland it is a place that visitors to Ireland never forget. Tralee is the capital town in Kerry, located in a quaint bay, which is at the head of The Dingle Peninsula; it is spectacularly beautiful and retains all it's charm of 800 years, as well as intriguing with all modern attractions.

Every year Tralee is the home of the Rose of Tralee festival, which is famed internationally for crowning some of the world's most beautiful women to be the Rose, a prestigious award.

Dingle is a hugely important commercial fishing centre in Ireland which, in more recent years it has become a much hugely popular nightspot among visitors to Ireland. Across the town there are Gift Shops, Hotels, pubs and restaurants. One of the main attractions to put Dingle on the map has been Fungi the Dolphin. Funghi has been a resident in Dingle for the past 30 years and has been embraced as part of the community by the locals. Local fishermen bring visitors out to catch a glimpse of him dashing through the water. Fungi's loyalty to the community has never waned. Once he even had his very own Dolphin girlfriend and still chose Dingle over swimming across the world with her.

The famous monk Brendan the navigator began his world famous voyage across the world from Dingle. In the surrounding areas of Dingle there are many other attractions including Dingle Crafts village, Blasket Islands heritage centre, Mount Brandon and Minard Castle.

The town of Listowel which dates back as far as the 12th century plays a key role in Irelands literary world. Every year Listowel is home to the Internationally renowned Writers Week. The festival encapsulates every aspect of the literary world from art to drama, music to storytelling. Listowel is also the home to what is referred to as The Garden of Europe - a shrub area, which is one of the only public monuments in the world, which is solely dedicated to the Holocaust. At the northeast centre of the square, which is the centre point of Listowel, is a plasterwork facade, which has been designed by Internationally known sculptor Patrick Mc Auliffe.

On the east shore of Lough Erne is Killarney. Founded by a man called Valentine Browne in the seventeenth century the village soon began to develop with the church as the focal point. The 4th Viscount of Kenmare Thomas Browne laid out the street plan for Killarney. The town has featured in many Hollywood classics including The Dawn, The Quiet Man, Far and Away and Ryan's Daughter. Sights worth visiting are The Franciscan Friary, The National Transport Museum and The Kerry Poets Memorial.

Day trips from Killarney are the Gap of Dunloe, A trip to Kenmare village, Killarney National Park, Ross's Island and Ross's Castle.

O'Connell St, Co. Limerick

County Limerick

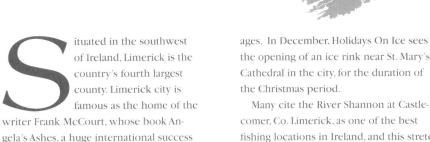

Church in Adare. Co. Limerick

Situated in the southwest of Ireland, Limerick is the country's fourth largest county. Limerick city is famous as the home of the writer Frank McCourt, whose book Angela's Ashes, a huge international success later made into a film, detailed his youth in what was then a poor city blighted by years of emigration and poverty. It has since undergone a face lift and today Limerick is a prosperous, international city that has seen a recent immigration boom.

Limerick International Poetry Festival takes place annually in Limerick City, and offers readings and workshops to suit all ages. In December, Holidays On Ice sees the opening of an ice rink near St. Mary's Cathedral in the city, for the duration of the Christmas period.

Many cite the River Shannon at Castlecomer, Co. Limerick, as one of the best fishing locations in Ireland, and this stretch of the river sees a generous run of salmon in the spring.

Visitors interested in Limerick's history should head to Limerick City Museum (recently renamed the Jim Kemmy Municipal Museum), which is home to all manner of artefacts including lace, bronze and iron ornaments and medieval coins.

Cottage in Adare. Co. Limerick

Old shop front. Co. Limerick

Counties Leitrim, Roscommon & Longford

The county of Leitrim offers the visitor mountains, lakes, rivers and unspoiled countryside.

The attractive town of Carrick-on-Shannon is a good place to start a cruise along the majestic River Shannon. Other popular activities in the area include golf, hill walking, angling and horse riding, and the perfect way to end your day is with Moon River, a company which offers a night out on the river, with traditional music and a lively atmosphere.

The Leitrim Way offers a walk from Lough Allen to the uplands of Barlear, during which you can experience the raw beauty of Leitrim first hand.

Also worth a visit is Glencar Waterfall. Set in a stunning location, this enchanting waterfall was the inspiration for William Butler Yeats' poem The Stolen Child.

Above: Leitrim, Parkes Castle, Lough Gill, below: Dromod

Roscommon boasts some spectacular scenery and is sometimes described as the hidden treasure of Ireland. The county is famous as the birthplace of the first Irish president, Douglas Hyde, who is commemorated at the Doctor Douglas Hyde Interpretative Centre in Frenchpark. The county is an ideal destination for visitors interested in history and scenic walks, and highlights include impressive stately homes such as King House and Clonalis House and the wonderful Lough Key Forest Park, one of the most extensive forest parks in Ireland.

Below: Longford Turf Cutting

The rivers and lakes in Longford offer visitors numerous outdoor activities. Whether you choose to go fishing on the River Shannon or walking along the shores of Lough Gowna, you shouldn't miss the county's stunning rural beauty.

Edgeworthstown House is famed for its adopted literary daughter, Maria Edgeworth. Although born in England, the writer lived much of her life in Edgeworthstown with her father, a local landowner. She dedicated her life's work to helping the local country people and assisted tirelessly during the Great Famine.

Edgeworthstown House has hosted many visitors over the years, including the poet William Wordsworth, and has also passed through the hands of a number of owners. Today, the great house is a nursing home.

Atlantic Drive, Co. Mayo

Counties Sligo & Mayo

Benbulben, Co.Sligo

Courtesy of Fáilte Ireland

Located in the north west of Ireland, Sligo is a county of great natural beauty, home to the famous Ben Bulben mountain (with its unusually flat top), a magnificent coastline and a number of golden beaches.

The county was one of the main emigration points during the Great Famine. However, this startlingly beautiful land is also associated with the poet William Butler Yeats and his brother, the artist Jack Yeats, who both spent time here and were influenced by the county's landscape. Lough Gill, near Sligo town, is home to the tiny island of Innisfree, immortalised in W.B. Yeats' celebrated poem, The Lake Isle of Innisfree. As children, the Yeats brothers visited the famous Lissadell House, owned by the Gore-Booth family. The most famous member of this clan was the Irish politician Countess Constance Markievicz, to whom W.B. Yeats remained close throughout his life. The poet is buried in Drumcliffe Graveyard, also in Sligo.

The county also offers a number of outdoor activities, and the seaside village of Rosses Point, with its two beaches and rolling surf, is a must for surfing enthusiasts.

The harbour here is marked by the Metal Man lighthouse, which guides seafarers safely through the surrounding waters.

There are some excellent walks in the Ox Mountains and the Knocknarea Mountains, about four miles south of Sligo town. At the top of Knocknarea Mountain is Queen Maeve's Cairn, which is thought to be the burial ground of this great warrior queen of Connacht.

A coastal county of stunning beauty, Mayo is the perfect place to get away from it all. Home to both busy towns and Blue Flag beaches, Mayo offers something for everyone. Off the Mayo coast, Achill Island offers unequalled views over the Atlantic as well as a healthy dose of traditional Irish music and entertainment. The Co. Mayo town of Ballina hosts the annual Ballina Street And Arts Festival, which features song, dance, art and literature. Also worth visiting is the holy mountain of Croagh Patrick near Westport, which sees thousands of pilgrims flock to climb it in honour of St. Patrick.

Offaly Clonmacnoise Temple Finan Round Tower

Counties Offaly, Laois & Kildare

Fashion at The Curragh Derby

The Curragh Derby   Courtesy of The Curragh Racecourse.

Offaly National Country Fair   Courtesy of Fáilte Ireland

Offaly has a wealth of cultural and historical attractions for visitors, including the monastic ruins in Clonmacnoise, the Georgian architecture in the town of Birr, the midland raised bog of Clara Bog Nature Reserve, and the Gothic buildings of Tullamore, the county town. Tullamore is famous for its whiskey, and the Whiskey Distillery Museum at the Tullamore Dew Heritage Centre offers interactive displays and is well worth a visit. Offaly also offers numerous outdoor activities, including walking in the beautiful Slieve Bloom mountains, golfing, cycling, and fishing.

This midlands county is home to thousands of historical sites and monuments. One of the principal archaeological sites in Ireland, the ancient, ruined fortifications of the Rock of Dunamase, near the town of Portlaoise, rise up from a flat plain – at a height of 46m, the rock was a highly strategic defensive position and commands impressive views right up to the beautiful Slieve Bloom Mountains. Laois also boasts a number of fine stately homes and gardens, including Emo Court Gardens and Ballaghmore Castle.

Situated to the west of Dublin, Kildare is famed for its wealth of sporting activities, including golf, hunting, horse racing and motor sport.

The Curragh Racecourse, located in the town of Newbridge, is Ireland's leading international horse racing venue and the home of the Irish Derby. Punchestown in the nearby town of Naas hosts another important horse racing event, the Irish National Hunt Festival. Established in 1850, this race meeting is held every April.

Golfing in Kildare is incredibly popular, and it is hard to find a town in the county that doesn't have a golf club. One of the finest is The K Club Hotel in Straffan, which has two 18-hole courses designed by Arnold Palmer. This luxurious location is perfect for a golfing holiday – and golf lessons are available for those who wish to brush up on their game. The K Club hosted the famous Ryder Cup competition in September 2006.

The Kildare Heritage and Genealogy Company, which can be found in the County Library in Newbridge, is an excellent resource for those wishing to trace their roots in the county – the centre offers access to documents including early Roman Catholic Records, which date back as far as 1753.

Kildare is also home to one of the four constituent universities that make up The National University of Ireland, in the picturesque town of Maynooth. This seat of learning was founded as The National College of St. Patrick in 1795.

Counties Kilkenny & Carlow

The name Kilkenny is derived from Cill Chainnigh, which means Church of Canice, after the 6th Century monk St. Canice who founded a monastery in Kilkenny city.

Set on the River Nore, Kilkenny Castle stands at the heart of this charming city. The original building, which was a wooden fortress rather than the stone castle which stands today, was constructed in the 12th Century. Parts of the present structure date back to the stone fortifications built in the 13th Century. The castle was the seat of the Butler family (the Dukes and Earls of Ormonde) for many centuries – in fact, it was only handed over to the State in the mid 20th Century. Parts of the castle are open to the public, as are its extensive gardens and woodlands.

Kilkenny is a centre for Irish crafts, and the city hosts a number of enjoyable festivals. Visitors will be enthralled by this small, medieval city's beauty and entertained by its lively nightlife.

Rich in history, Co. Kilkenny is peppered with medieval ruins, ancient stone walls, picturesque villages and a number of historic structures, including Jerpoint Abbey in Thomastown, a beautiful 12th Century Cistercian abbey.

The town of Rathvilly was the home to volunteer Kevin Barry, who fought for Irish freedom but was captured and executed in Dublin aged just 18. His life is remembered in the song The Ballad of Kevin Barry.

Rich in ecclesiastical and cultural history, Carlow offers plenty to see and do. Activities on offer include walking in Altamount House and Gardens in Tullow, golfing in Borris, and exploring the historical remains of Carlow Castle in Carlow town.

The town of Rathvilly was the home to volunteer Kevin Barry, who fought for Irish freedom but was captured and executed in Dublin aged just 18. His life is remembered in the song The Ballad of Kevin Barry.

Carlow Castlle, River Barrow

River Barrow

Above: Kilkenny Castle, below: Kilkenny Cathedral

Above: Carlow Altamont House Garden, below: Kilkenny High St.

County Tipperary

Home to the Galtee Mountains and the Glen of Aherlow, the scenic county of Tipperary has a proud sporting tradition, and offers a huge range of outdoor activities, including hurling, horse racing, golf and water sports.

Tipperary is renowned for its hospitality, so visitors are assured of a warm welcome. A must-see attraction is The Rock of Cashel, an impressive set of medieval buildings set on an outcrop of limestone. Those looking for a more energetic way to spend a day should head to the Equestrian Centre and Mitchelstown Cave in Cahir, and a number of walking tours are available throughout the county, providing an excellent way to enjoy the stunning scenery.

Fine dining and luxurious accommodation can be found at the stylish Cashel Palace Hotel, which is set in 28 acres of charming gardens

Rock of Cashel, Co. Tipperary

above: Cruising on the River Shannon, North Tipperary, below right: Rock of Cashel, below left: Ormonde Castle, Co.Tipperary

Counties Fermanagh & Tyrone

Lough Erne, Co. Fermanagh

Lough Erne in Fermanagh is a popular boating destination for visitors to Ireland. Situated in the very centre of the lough is the attractive market town of Enniskillen. It is an ideal place to stop over for a night or two and do a bit of investigating. Worth seeing when in Enniskillen is The Portora Royal School, which was attended by two of Ireland's greatest literary figures, Oscar Wilde and Samuel Beckett.

Set on the banks of the River Erne, Enniskillen Castle was first constructed by the Gaelic Chieftain Hugh Maguire in the 15th Century. Today, the castle's museums provide a wealth of information about Fermanagh's history, wildlife and landscape, and exhibitions and events are held throughout the year.

Fermanagh is home to one of the most beautiful country houses in Ireland, Florence Court. This 18th Century Irish Palladian mansion was the brainchild of John Cole, and the house was named after his wife Florence. Much of the present structure was built by Cole's son, later the first Lord Mount Florence. The house boasts some impressive historical features, including the embellished rococo plasterwork of the dining room and some beautifully preserved 19th Century beds and a writing cabinet. The mansion offers wonderful views of the surrounding mountains, and there is a recently restored water-powered sawmill in the grounds. The house is open to the public, and a tour visits all rooms as well the mansion's gardens and the forest park close by. The tour also provides an insight into the Cole Family, who established the house when they moved to Ireland from Devon.

Close to Florence House are The Marble Arch Caves. The caves were carved out of the limestone terrain by streams that flow down the barren slopes of the Cuilcagh Mountains. The streams flow underground and form the Claddagh River – a tour of the caves takes you along this underground river by boat, passing waterfalls, narrow passages and high-ceilinged chambers full of stalactites and stalagmites.

Above: Florence Court, Co. Fermanagh, below, Gortin Valley, Co. Tyrone

A largely rural county rich in bogland, rivers and lakes, Tyrone is one of the six counties that make up Northern Ireland.

Situated in the town of Dungannon, the Tyrone Crystal Shop and Visitor Centre offers guided tours in which you can see the crystal making process at firsthand, and there's also the opportunity to purchase souvenirs from the craft centre.

Gortin Glen Forest Park is just north of the town of Omagh. It was first opened in 1967, and although originally planted for timber production, it is now a major recreational area where visitors can enjoy camping, horse riding and orienteering, as well as the breathtaking surrounding scenery.

The town of Clogher was the 5th Century seat of the oldest bishopric in Ireland, and was visited by Oliver Plunkett in the 17th Century. The Clogher Valley Railway was first used in 1887 and closed in 1941 – the town's charming station is now a coffee house. The famous Clogher Valley Show takes place annually in the area and offers local farm produce, including the well-known Clogher Valley Cheese.

Counties Waterford & Wexford

Situated in the south east of the country, Waterford is internationally renowned for its handcrafted crystal. The Waterford Crystal Visitors Centre in Waterford city offers a fascinating tour on which visitors can see the crystal making process, and souvenir hunters can choose from a range of beautiful crystal gifts in the centre's shop.

Coastal towns such as Dunmore East and Tramore offer unspoiled beaches and attractive scenery. Both are popular holiday resorts, with entertainment for all the family. On the coast not far from Tramore are three tall concrete pillars standing in a field. Built after a tragedy that saw hundreds of people lose their lives when a transport ship went down in Tramore Bay in 1816, the pillars are a warning to seafarers in the rocky bay below. On top of one of the pillars stands the statue known as the Metal Man – who, according to legend, bellows out warnings on stormy evenings.

Located in the south east of Ireland, Wexford boasts a scenic coastline and has long been a popular destination for visitors. Originally a prehistoric settlement, today Wexford town is a thriving place with some beautifully preserved historical architecture. The Irish name for Wexford is Loch Gorman, a name that derives from the legend of Garman Grabh, who is claimed to have drowned in the mudflats of the harbour. The Vikings originally referred to Wexford as 'Waestfjord', meaning 'harbour of the mudflats'.

When the ancient cartographer Ptolemy mapped out Wexford he called it Menapia, after a tribe which originated in Belgium and travelled there in prehistoric times. In 1169, the Normans invaded Wexford and the first-ever Irish treaty was signed at Selkar Abbey. In 1649, Cromwell entered Wexford City and it is said that as many as 200 Wexford inhabitants died at the hands of his troops.

Sights worth seeing in Wexford town include St. Iberius Church, The West Gate, and The Burning Bush Tabernacle. A number of excursions leave from Wexford town, and destinations on offer include the Irish Agriculture Museum, the Irish National Heritage Park, Ladies Island and the Salty Islands.

*Above: The Clocktower, Co. Waterford
below: Wexford Harbour*

Above: Waterford Cathedral, right: tall ship race off Dunmore East, below: Ferrycarrig, Co.Wexford

Above, Powerscourt Waterfalls; Below Right, Bray Coastline; Below Left, Blessington Lakes, Co Wicklow

Courtesy of Colm Moody

County Wicklow

Powerscourt House, Enniskerry, Co. Wicklow

The landscape of Wicklow is marked by mountains, lakes and a beautiful coastline, all of which combine to provide some of the most stunning views in Ireland. The county is known as The Garden of Ireland, due to a mild and moist climate that encourages the growth of many types of plants and trees. A popular hiking destination, the Wicklow mountains are rich in wildlife and peppered with bogs and rivers.

Vikings arrived in the area in the 9th Century and set up a trading port in what is now Wicklow town.

The English name of Wicklow derives from the Danish moniker 'Wyking-alo', meaning 'Viking meadow'. In the 12th Century, the Anglo Normans invaded and the town of Wicklow was granted to a nobleman by the name of Maurice Fitzgerald.

Situated on the N11 road linking Dublin to Wexford, Avoca is a picturesque village in which the popular BBC television show Ballykissangel was filmed. The valley of Avoca was always rich in minerals from copper to gold – some of the gold coins found there are now on display in Dublin's National Museum. Now a highly successful business, Avoca Handweavers was founded in 1723 in Avoca village. Situated on the banks of the Avoca River, the company's watermill dates back to the early 18th Century and is the oldest of its kind in Ireland. It is still used in the weaving of many of the products available to buy in the company's shops. The Avoca Handweavers shop offers a great range of unique products, including clothes, accessories, books, plants and gadgets, and the firm also exports its goods worldwide. Complete your visit with a trip to the company's café to sample its delicious lunches and home baking.

Wicklow town and the seaside resort of Bray offer lively nightlife, and some of the county's quaint pubs stage live traditional music. Wicklow also hosts the annual Garden Festival from May until August, during which visitors can see a variety of public and private gardens.

From the breathtaking formal gardens at Powerscourt to the amusements in Bray to the pretty villages of Greystones and Avoca, Wicklow is a county that offers something for everyone.

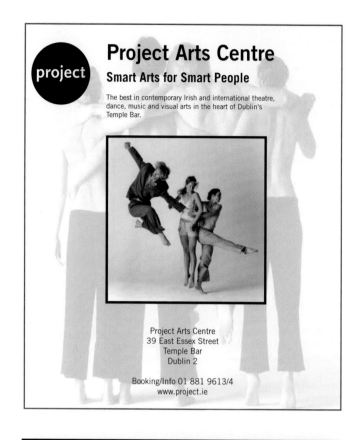

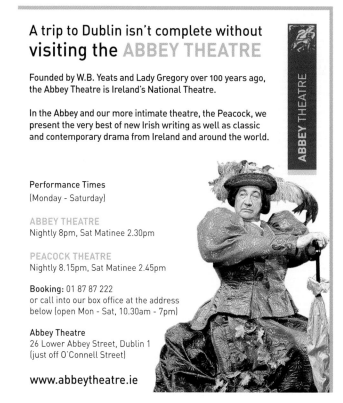

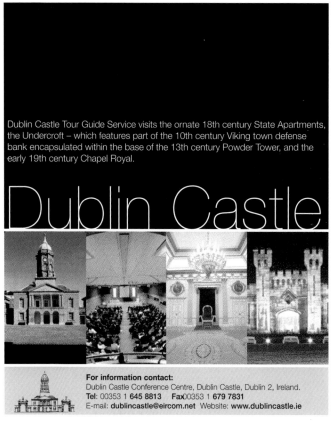

The Old Jameson Distillery, Dublin

Discover for yourself how Jameson became the world's favourite Irish Whiskey!
Guided tours: 9.30 a.m. – 6.00 p.m. (last tour at 5.30 p.m.) Open 7 days

Also at the Distillery

"The Still Room Restaurant":
Serving light lunches and the most
memorable of Irish Coffees!

"1780" Public Bar
The perfect spot to enjoy an afternoon
or evening of easy relaxation with friends.
(Lunch served 12.00 p.m. – 2.30 p.m.)

Jameson Gift & Whiskey Shop

The Old Jameson Distillery,
Bow Street,
Smithfield, Dublin 7
E: reservations@ojd.ie

www.jamesondistillery.ie

Uncover the secret to Jameson's smoothness!

Laughter Lounge

Bookings: 1800 266 339

Visit www.laughterlounge.com to see what special guest will appear in the autumn.

The Laughter Lounge Comedy Club
4 - 8 Eden Quay
O'Connell Bridge
Dublin 1
Web: www.laughterlounge.com
Email: info@laughterlounge.com
Tickets €20 (Students €15)
Ticketmaster www.ticketmaster.ie

The Laughter Lounge is back on its original home on Eden Quay, O'Connell Bridge. Three years in development the all-new Laughter Lounge opened its door again in February 2006 and is now firmly centre-stage as Ireland's premier comedy venue.

Bill Bailey, Tommy Tiernan, Jo Brand, Dara O'Briain, Phil Jupitus, Des Bishop, Johnny Vegas, Ardal O'Hanlon, Rich Hall, Whose Line is it anyway? The Laughter Lounge has played host to some of the world's top international comedians.

The Laughter Lounge is open to the public every Thursday, Friday & Saturday with a different line up each week for individual, small or large group bookings. It is advisable to book well in advance to guarantee the date you want, as the comedy nights are very popular.

Each night the venue with its two fully licensed bars and intimate cabaret seating arrangements hosts 4 of the best Irish and international comedians, together for a hilarious two hour show catering for a variety of tastes and age groups, we only book the best!

No need to rush off after the show into the cold, dark outside world of nightclub queues and bouncers as our resident DJ Toby Sinclair and late bar license will keep you smiling on the dance floor till late.

The Lighthouse B&B
The High Road, Ballinaboula,
Dingle, Co. Kerry
Phone (066) 915 18 29
info@lighthousedingle.com
www.lighthousedingle.com

The Lighthouse B&B

The Lighthouse is a family run B&B commanding wonderful views of Dingle Harbour.
In business now for eight years, The Lighthouse offers a friendly welcome and guarantees a comfortable nights stay. Twin double and family rooms available with complimentary tea or coffee, all rooms are en suite.
Proprietors, Mary and Denis Murphy are always on hand to offer advice to the visitor on sightseeing or good places to go for dinner.

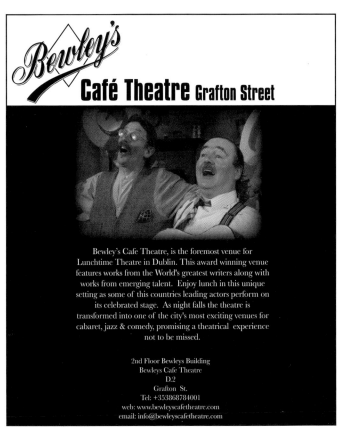

Bewley's
Café Theatre Grafton Street

Bewley's Cafe Theatre, is the foremost venue for Lunchtime Theatre in Dublin. This award winning venue features works from the World's greatest writers along with works from emerging talent. Enjoy lunch in this unique setting as some of this countries leading actors perform on its celebrated stage. As night falls the theatre is transformed into one of the city's most exciting venues for cabaret, jazz & comedy, promising a theatrical experience not to be missed.

2nd Floor Bewleys Building
Bewleys Cafe Theatre
D.2
Grafton St.
Tel: +353868784001
web: www.bewleyscafetheatre.com
email: info@bewleyscafetheatre.com

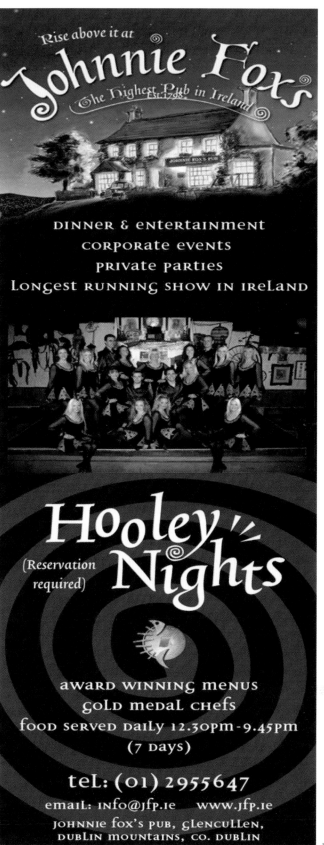

Rise above it at
Johnnie Foxs
The Highest Pub in Ireland Est. 1798.

DINNER & ENTERTAINMENT
CORPORATE EVENTS
PRIVATE PARTIES
LONGEST RUNNING SHOW IN IRELAND

Hooley Nights
(Reservation required)

award winning menus
gold medal chefs
food served daily 12.30pm - 9.45pm
(7 days)

tel: (01) 2955647
email: info@jfp.ie   www.jfp.ie

johnnie fox's pub, glencullen,
dublin mountains, co. dublin

POWERSCOURT
HOUSE & GARDENS

ONE OF EUROPE'S GREATEST GARDENS
ONE OF IRELAND'S GREATEST TREASURES

Speciality Shops - Terrace Cafe – Exhibition - Garden Pavilion

Open 7 days 9.30am to 5.30pm – Located 20kms South of Dublin
Enniskerry, Co. Wicklow Tel: 01 204 6000 Fax: 01 204 6900
www.powerscourt.ie

POWERSCOURT
GOLF CLUB

One magnificent setting, two magnificent courses.
Visitors are always welcome every day of the week.

Enniskerry, Co. Wicklow Tel: 01 204 6033 Fax: 01 276 1303
www.powerscourt.ie

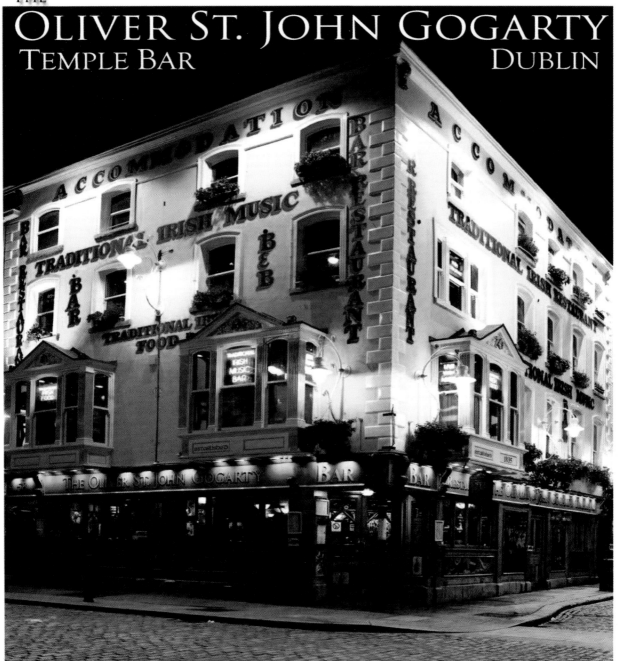

THE OLIVER ST. JOHN GOGARTY
TEMPLE BAR — DUBLIN

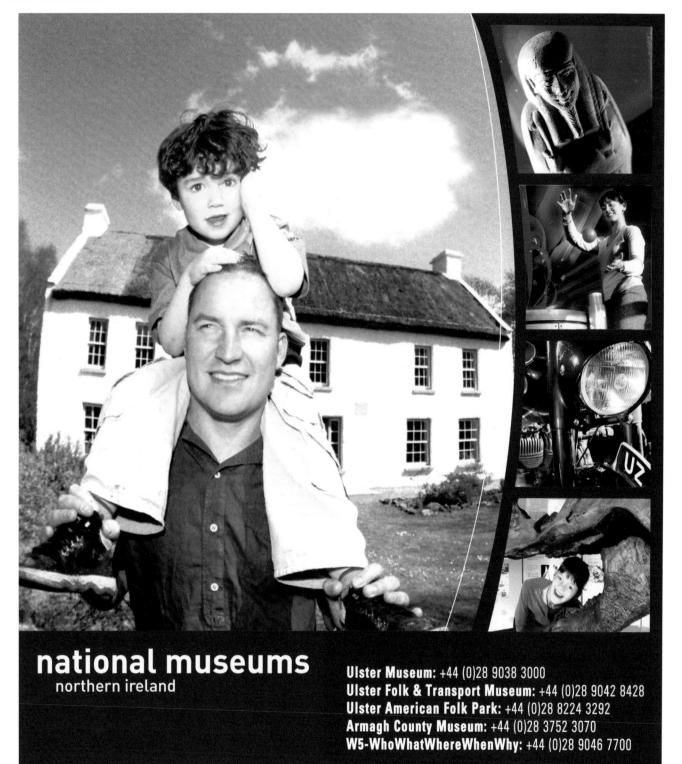

national museums
northern ireland

Ulster Museum: +44 (0)28 9038 3000
Ulster Folk & Transport Museum: +44 (0)28 9042 8428
Ulster American Folk Park: +44 (0)28 8224 3292
Armagh County Museum: +44 (0)28 3752 3070
W5-WhoWhatWhereWhenWhy: +44 (0)28 9046 7700

Project supported by the
EU Programme
for Peace and Reconciliation

Northern Ireland
Tourist Board

www.magni.org.uk

OPW
The Office of Public Works
Oifig na nOibreacha Poiblí

Heritage Sites of Ireland

One of responsibilities the Office of Public Works (OPW) is the protection, conservation and presentation of Ireland's built heritage. Many millions from Ireland and overseas visit these heritage sites each year to learn something of Ireland's history and heritage.

While many of you will be familiar with places like the Rock of Cashel, Dublin Castle and Newgrange I would like to draw your attention to other lesser known sites throughout Ireland. Indeed you need only travel a couple of hours at most to find and enjoy these gems.

Our highly praised guide service will bring these places to life to further enhance your experience.

For further information call
+353 (0)1 6476593

For information on the OPW heritage card call
+353 (0)1 6476587

OPW
The Office of Public Works
Oifig na nOibreacha Poiblí

Heritage Sites of Ireland

Carrowmore Megalithic Cemetery
Sligo
This is the largest cemetery of megalithic tombs in Ireland and is also among the country's oldest. Over 60 tombs have been located by archaeologists, the oldest pre-date Newgrange by some 700 years. A restored cottage houses a small exhibition relating to the site.
Restricted access in centre for people with disabilities (Tombs are inaccessible to people with disabilities).
Visitors are advised to wear shoes suitable for walking on uneven terrain.
Open Easter to end October
Daily 10.00-18.00
Tel: +353 (0)71 916 1534

Parke's Castle
Fivemile Bourne, Leitrim
Restored plantation castle of the early 17th century. Open March to October
Tel: +353 (0)71 9164149

Boyle Abbey
Boyle, Co. Roscommon
A Cistercian monastery found in the 12th century.
Open Easter-end October daily 10.00-18.00. Tel: +353 (0)71 9662604

Ferns Castle
Ferns, Co. Wexford
The castle was built in the 13th century. Only half of the castle now remains. The most complete tower contains a fine circular chapel, with carved ornament.
Tel: +353 (0)54 66411

Trim Castle
Trim, Co. Meath
Trim Castle is the largest Anglo-Norman castle in Ireland. Construction of the massive three storied Keep was begun c.1176.
Tel: +353 (0)46 9438619

Castletown
Celbridge, Co. Kildare
Castletown is the most significant Palladian style country house in Ireland. Built c.1722, it features designs by Alessandro Galilei, Sir Edward Lovett Pearce and Sir William Chambers.
Tel: +353 (0)1 628 8252

Céide Fields
Ballycastle, Co. Mayo
Stone Age landscape of stone-walled fields, dwellings and megalithic tombs over 5,000 years old. Open Mid-Mar-Nov daily. Tel: +353 (0)96 43325

www.heritageireland.ie

135

Heritage Sites of Ireland

Brú na Bóinne Vistor Centre (Newgrange and Knowth) (UNESCO World Heritage site)

Donore, Co. Meath

Brú na Bóinne Visitor Centre, open in 1997, is designed to present the archaeological heritage of the Boyne Valley, which includes the megalithic passage tombs of Newgrange and Knowth. The Centre is the starting point for all visits to both monuments, and contains extensive interpretative displays and viewing areas.

All visitors wishing to visit Newgrange and Knowth must begin their visit at the Visitor Centre. There is no direct access to these monuments. All admission tickets are issued at Brú na Bóinne Visitor Centre.

Please note that this is a very busy site and visitors must expect a delay in the summer months if visiting Newgrange and Knowth and access is not guaranteed. Groups which have pre-booked are expected at Brú na Bóinne Visitor Centre at the appointed time, not at the monuments.

For further information on opening times and facilities please contact +353 (0)41 9880300.

Ormond Castle

Carrick-on-Suir, Co. Tipperary
Ormond Castle is the best example of an Elizabethan manor house in Ireland. It was built by Thomas, the 10th Earl of Ormond in the 1560s.
Tel: +353 (0)51 640787

Old Mellifont Abbey

Tullyallen, Drogheda, Co. Meath
The first Cistercian monastery in Ireland founded in 1142 by St. Malachy of Armagh. Its most unusual feature is the octagonal Lavabo c.1200.
Tel: +353 (0)41 982 6459

Glendalough

Glendalough, Co. Wicklow
This early Christian monastic site was founded by St. Kevin in the 6th century. The monastic remains include a superb round tower, stone churches and decorated crosses.
Tel: +353 (0)404 45325/45352

www.heritageireland.ie

OPW
The Office of Public Works
Oifig na nOibreacha Poiblí

CROKE PARK STADIUM
PÁIRC AN CHRÓCAIGH

Team Work

A unique conference and event solution combining a spectacular venue and luxury accommodation in a central Dublin location

- 87 meeting rooms for up to 75 people theatre style
- Exhibition and conference suites for up to 800 theatre style
- 4-star Jurys Croke Park Hotel with 232 bedrooms, executive
- lounge & business centre
- GAA Museum & Croke Park Stadium Tours
- 7.5km from Dublin airport / 1km from city centre
- Free car parking

Quotations & Enquiries

t: 01 819 2300 • e: events@crokepark.ie • w: www.crokepark.ie

John M Keating

Bar | Café | Restaurant

The former St. Mary's Church, Junction of Mary St. & Jervis St., Dublin1

Historical Figures Associated with the former St. Mary's Church:

Arthur Guinness - Founder of the Guinness Brewery
Seán O'Casey - Playwright & Author of 'The Plough & The Stars'
Theobald Wolfe Tone - United Irishmen Founder
Richard Brinsley Sheridan – Playwright & Author of 'School for Scandal'
Jonathan Swift - Author of 'Gulliver's Travels' and Dean of St. Patrick's Cathedral
The Earl of Charlemont - Irish Volunteer

Late Bar with DJ until 2.30am every Friday & Saturday
Classical String Quartet Saturday & Sunday afternoon
Tower Bar with plasma screen for major sporting events
Outdoor Terrace Bar & Café

Reservations: **087 636 3738 / 01 828 0102**   Email: **restaurant@jmk.ie**   Website: **www.jmk.ie**

LAPELLO

IRELANDS PREMIER GENTLEMAN'S CLUB

141

We've always been famous for food and drink. In 2006, we'll be famous for golf too.

With the Ryder Cup coming to Ireland in September 2006, there's no better time to remind you of another prestigious Irish phenomenon – our food and drink industry. In a constantly evolving world market, Irish food and drink companies are thriving.

Take our world–renowned alcoholic beverage industry. Representing almost 10% of the country's overall food and drink output, production of alcoholic drinks is valued in excess of $2.2 billion at factory prices. It's a cornerstone of our economy. In addition to the well–known international companies and brands, recent years have seen the rise of a burgeoning independent sector, engaged both in private label supply and the development of new branded products. Find out more about them, and plenty more successful food and drink companies like them, by visiting Ireland The Food Island at our website.

Ireland
THE FOOD ISLAND
www.foodisland.com

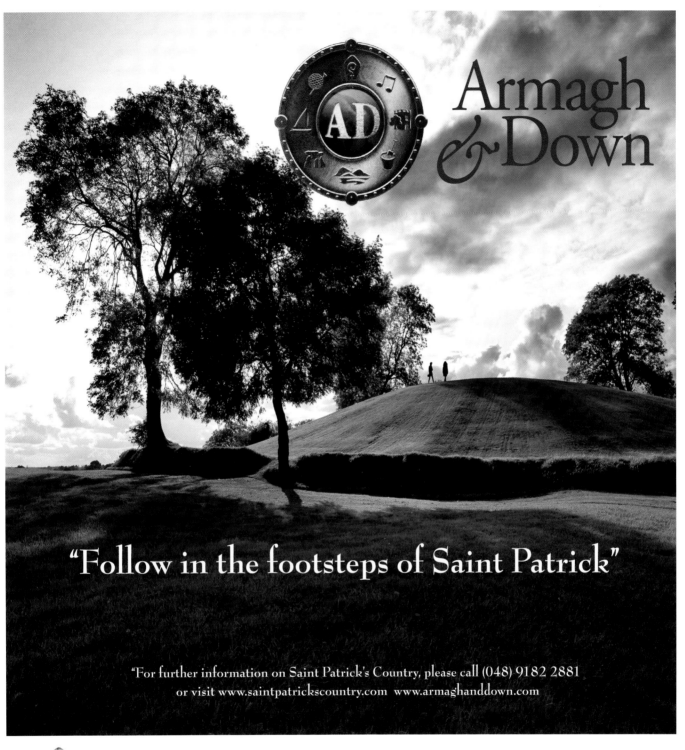

"Follow in the footsteps of Saint Patrick"

"For further information on Saint Patrick's Country, please call (048) 9182 2881
or visit www.saintpatrickscountry.com www.armaghanddown.com

143

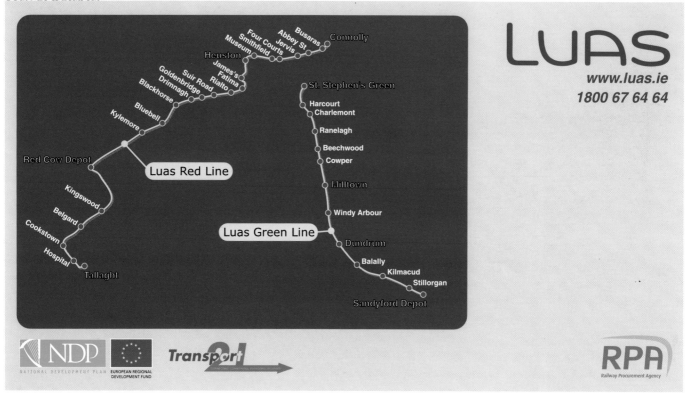

"In business, you don't get what you deserve,
you get what you negotiate."

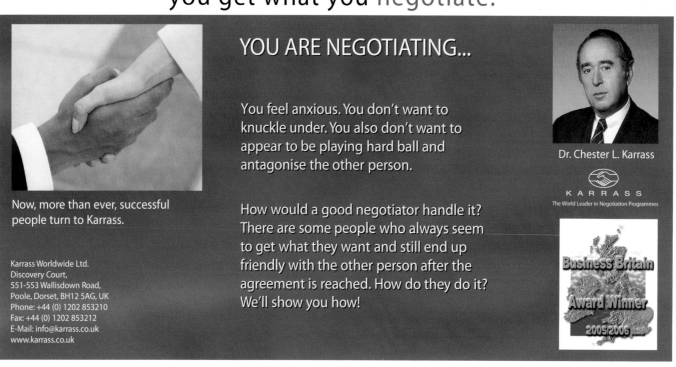

©2006 Delta Air Lines Inc.

CROSSING DAILY

DUBLIN/SHANNON TO NEW YORK

Delta
SKYTEAM
delta.com

Delta Air Lines is now flying daily from Dublin and Shannon to New York (JFK) as well as to Atlanta. This gives you convenient connections to over 170 destinations in the U.S., Latin America and the Caribbean.

For further information please call 1850 88 2031, visit our website or contact your local travel agent.

A Day to Remember

Welcome to Waterford. Enjoy the Experience.

Factory Tour
Retail Store
Craft & Jewellery Giftstore

WATERFORD
CRYSTAL
VISITOR CENTRE™

Gatchell's Restaurant
World Wide Shipping
Global Refund

OPENING HOURS

RETAIL STORE	FACTORY TOUR
Jan & Feb, Nov & Dec 7 days Mon-Sun 9.00am - 5.00pm	Jan & Feb, Nov & Dec 5 days Mon-Fri 9.00am - 3.15pm *(last tour)*
March to October incl. 7 days Mon-Sun 8.30am - 6.00pm	March to October incl. 7 days Mon-Sun 8.30am - 4.00pm *(last tour)*

FOR INFORMATION: T: +353 51 332500 F: +353 51 332716 E: visitorreception@waterford.ie www.waterfordvisitorcentre.com

ACCOMMODATION
THE LIGHTHOUSE B&B

TEL:	+ 353 (0)66 915 18 29
WEB:	www.lighthousedingle.com
ADDRESS:	The High Road, Ballinaboula, Dingle, Co. Kerry
EMAIL:	info@lighthousedingle.com

The Lighthouse is a family run B&B commanding wonderful views of Dingle Harbour. In business now for eight years, The Lighthouse offers a friendly welcome and guarantees a comfortable nights stay. Twin double and family rooms available with complimentary tea or coffee, all rooms are en suite. Proprietors, Mary and Denis Murphy are always on hand to offer advice to the visitor on sightseeing or good places to go for dinner.

ANGLING
KINSALE ANGLING

WEB:	www.kinsaleangling.com
ADDRESS:	1 Rampart Lane, The Ramparts, Kinsale, Co Cork
TEL:	+ 353 (0)21 4774946

From simply meeting you at the marina for your very first day's fishing, to organizing the complete package for groups of professional anglers from point of arrival to point of return - we do it all. We want to help get the most from this great sport and relaxing pastime.

ENTERTAINMENT
LOUIS MULCAHY VISITOR CENTRE

WEB:	www.louismulcahy.com
ADDRESS:	Clogher, Ballyferriter, Dingle, Kerry.
TEL:	+ 353 (0)66 9156229

After nearly thirty years of customer's requests to be allowed see the work in progress or try their hand at throwing a pot, Louis Mulcahy has dedicated an area at the pottery to those visitors who wish to experience the craft for themselves. This Visitor Centre is open 7 days a week (Easter to September) Monday - Friday (October - Easter) from 10am - 5pm

GALLERY
CHESTER BEATTY LIBRARY

WEB:	www.cbl.ie
ADDRESS:	Dublin Castle, Dublin 2
TEL:	+353 (0))1 407 0750

Chester Beatty

European Museum of the Year 2002, the Chester Beatty Library is an art museum and library which houses Sir Alfred Chester Beatty's great collection of manuscripts, miniature paintings, prints, drawings, rare books and decorative arts from countries across Asia, the Middle East, North Africa and Europe. A visual feast for visitors, the exhibitions open a window on the artistic treasures of the great cultures and religions of the world.

GALLERY
DALKEY ARTS GALLEY

ADDRESS:	19 Railway Rd, Dalkey Co. Dublin
WEB:	www.dalkeyarts.com
EMAIL:	info@dalkeyarts.com
TEL:	+353 (0)1 284 9663
FAX:	+353 (0)1 284 9663

Dalkey Arts Gallery is a cutting edge gallery with 18 years experience in the art and framing industry. We represent fresh Irish and international artists both established and up and coming talent. Oil & watercolour paintings, drawings, prints and sculpture. We can package and ship to anywhere in the world. Hours: Monday to Saturday 10 to 6pm, Sunday and Bank Holidays 1 to 6pm, and by appointment.

GALLERY
NATIONAL GALLERY OF IRELAND

WEB:	www.nationalgallery.ie
ADDRESS:	Merrion Square, Dublin 2.
TEL:	+ 353 (0)1 661 5133

The National Gallery of Ireland houses the national collection of Irish art and European master paintings. Admission to the permanent collection is free.

GALLERY
SOLOMON GALLERY

WEB:	www.solomongallery.com
ADDRESS:	Powerscourt Townhouse Centre, South William Street, Dublin2
TEL:	+ 353 (0)1 6794237
FAX:	+ 353 (0)1 6715262
EMAIL:	info@solomongallery.com

The Solomon was established in 1981 and is one of Ireland's leading contemporary art galleries.
The Solomon is conveniently located in Dublin City Centre. The gallery has built it's reputation on representing Irish and international artists working primarily in a figurative style. In addition of hosting regular contemporary exhibitions, the Solomon also deals in investment and collectible art by important Irish and British Artists. Opening hours: Mon – Sat 10am - 5.30pm PETER COLLIS RHA, KITCHEN STILL LIFE, OIL ON CANVAS,12" X 12"

GALLERY
THE ROYAL HIBERNIAN GALLERY

ADDRESS:	Gallagher Gallery, 15 Ely Place, Dublin 2
TEL:	00353 (0)1 661 2558
WEB:	www.royalhibernianacademy.ie
ADDRESS:	rhagallery1@eircom.net
FAX:	00353 (0) 661 0762

The R.H.A Gallagher Gallery is the principal public art gallery in the city centre, within 5 minutes walk of St Stephens Green, dedicated to developing, affirming and challenging the public's appreciation and understanding of traditional and innovative approaches to the visual arts.

John Gerrard, Smoke Tree III, 2006, Realtime 3D, 117 x 68 x 53 cm / variable, Collection Hilger Contemporary, Vienna

GALLERY
CLEGGAN BEACH RIDING CENTRE

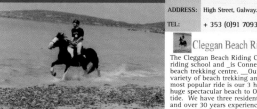

WEB:	www.kennysirishbookshop.ie
ADDRESS:	High Street, Galway.
TEL:	+ 353 (0)91 709350

Cleggan Beach Riding Centre

The Cleggan Beach Riding Centre is an approved riding school and _is Connemara's most renowned beach trekking centre. _Our facilities include a variety of beach trekking and mountain treks. Our most popular ride is our 3 hour trek across a huge spectacular beach to Omey Island at low tide. We have three resident qualified instructors, and over 30 years experience. We have well-schooled horses and ponies suitable for all ages and standards.

HORSE RIDING
KILLARNEY RIDING STABLES

WEB:	www.horsevactionireland.com
ADDRESS:	Ballydowney, Killarney.
TEL:	+ 353 (0)64 31686

Killarney Riding Stables & Paddocks Accommodation is located just 1 mile from the heart of Killarney town and adjacent to the Killarney National Park.
We are Irish Tourist Board and Association of Irish Riding Establishments approved. Established in the late 1960's, the stables can expertly provide each and every customer with a unique experience.

HORSE RIDING
THE CONNEMARA AND COAST TRAILS

WEB:	www.aille-cross.com
ADDRESS:	Loughrea, Co Galway
TEL:	+353 (0)91 841216

The Connemara Trail is not just for riders, but for anyone who enjoys activities in a peaceful Irish atmosphere. On demand, many activities such as river fishing and deep-sea fishing, golf, cycling, mountain climbing or walking the little deserted roads, swimming etc. can be organised. Non-riders will meet their riding Partners every evening to share their daily experience in the hotel pub.

PARAGLIDING
MIDLAND PARAGLIDING

WEB:	www.midlandparagliding.com
ADDRESS:	6 Cashel Road, Tipperary Town, Tipperary.
TEL:	+ 353 (0)62 52429

At Midland Paragliding we are committed to making sure your flying with us is a fabulous experience where your safety is paramount. Training is usually conducted on gentle nursery slopes, practising take offs and 'low hops', all the time under our expert tuition. All our instructors are very experienced pilots with a caring and enthusiastic attitude committed to maximising your enjoyment and safe progress.

SHOOTING
COURTLOUGH SHOOTING GROUNDS

TEL:	00353 (01) 841 3096

WEB:	www.courtlough.ie
ADDRESS:	Courtlough Cork City, Ireland
EMAIL:	info@courtlough.ie

Courtlough Shooting grounds ,established in 1996 by former Irish Olympian and former team member Richard Flynn and his son William also an Irish team member.
Since 1996 Courtlough has expanded to become the premier shooting grounds in the Country. Courtlough currently operates on 23 acres of land and the facility can cater for up to 200 guests per day.

SHOPPING
CELTIC WHISKEY SHOP

TEL:	+ 00 353 68 21074
ADDRESS:	227-28 Dawson Street, Dublin 2

WEB:	www.celticwhiskeyshop.com
FAX:	+ 00 353 (0)1 675 9768
EMAIL:	ally@celticwhiskeyshop.com

The Celtic Whiskey Shop, located in the heart of Dublin's shopping centre, is one of the city's treasure troves, with the largest selection of Irish whiskey in the world, as well as a huge range of world whiskeys and spirits. Knowledgeable staff are happy to guide visitors through the range, and free whiskey tastings are available instore everyday. CWS offer a word-wide shipping service, and orders can be placed instore or at www.celticwhiskeyshop.com. Slainte!

SHOPPING
KILKENNY SHOP

TEL:	+ 353 (0)1 677 7066

WEB:	www.kilkennyshop.com
ADDRESS:	5/6 Nassau Street, Dublin 2. 6/7 High Street, Co. Galway 3 New Street, Killarney, Co. Kerry

KILKENNY stores are synonymous with the finest of Irish design in contemporary fashion and gifts. The stores serve as a showcase for both new and established designers in clothing, crystal, jewellery, pottery and crafts. Gifts for all occasions are our speciality! We also provide a wedding list service, corporate gifts, hampers and much much more.

SHOPPING
LOUIS MULCAHY POTTERY

ADDRESS:	46 Dawson St, Dublin 2.

WEB:	www.louismulcahy.com
ADDRESS:	dublin@louismulcahy.com
TEL:	+353 (0)1 6709311

At his studio/workshop in Ballyferriter on the Dingle Peninsula, Louis Mulcahy designs and makes the very best Irish craft Pottery in exquisite fine porcelain and robust stoneware. A browse through the Dawson Street (South Anne St. Corner) shop is a pleasant unhassled experience, thanks to the discreet, friendly staff.

SHOPPING
STEPHEN'S GREEN SHOPPING CENTRE

WEB:	www.stephensgreen.com
ADDRESS:	Stephen's Green, Dublin 2
TEL:	+ 353 (0)1 478 0888

Work began on the Stephen's Green Shopping Centre in 1985, with the whole project taking 36 months to complete. The centre opened it's doors on the 8th November, 1988 and has gone from strength to strength. Located in the heart of the city at the top of Grafton Street, Dublin's best known and busiest thoroughfare, you'll find everything you need in fashion and footwear, food and plenty of great gift ideas here.

SIGHTSEEING
CHRIST CHURCH CATHEDRAL

ADDRESS:	Christchurch place, Dublin 8
TEL:	+353 (0)1 679 8991

WEB:	www.cccdub.ie
EMAIL:	welcome@cccdub.ie
FAX:	+353 (0)1 677 8099

Re-built at the investigation of the Norman Knight, Richard de Clare, {Strongbow} and Archbishop Lorcan Ua Tuathail (St. Laurence O'Toole) around 1170 on the site of an earlier Viking wooden cathedral dating from c.1030. Rebuilt in the mid-16th. Century and extensively restored between 1871-78, the Cathedral has a splendid lofty interior with stone vaulting and the largest crypt in Ireland. This was used as a market for beer, wine and tobacco until at least 1670 and now houses an exhibition of church treasures. The embalmment of St Laurence is enshrined in the St. Laud chapel.

Index

FeaturesPhotographer

Kevin Morris

Kevin Morris has been a photographer for the last twenty or so years and in 2006 decided to take the steps towards setting up his own photography business. It seems that photography is something that runs through his veins, his father, Louglin Morris, was one of Dublin's most celebrated photographers throughout the 60's and 70's. Kevin's main interest, and first love, is in landscape photography, and he has one of those rare talents which is so hard to find.

As a keen family man, Kevin's hometown is beautiful Donabate Co Dublin, a photographers Mecca. Kevin thoroughly enjoys travelling to the local sites and capturing their true beauty. When time and work permits, he likes to travel further afield to build up his library of images from around Ireland. His pictures have been used in some of 2006's calendars aiming to capture the essence of Ireland, as well as property brochures for local developments..

With an extensive and admirable portfolio, Kevin covers all aspects of photography. Kevin sells framed prints of both well known, and obscure, landmarks which make for an ideal gift for loved ones abroad or even for those who wish to have a permanent reminder of their stay in beautiful Ireland. He has also recently moved into the digital art area, using sunrises & sunsets to create spectacular images which are proving very popular with clients. His web site is www.kevinmorris.ie and well worth checking out.

Contact details:
Phone 01 8436953 / 087 1369620
Email : kevinpmorris@gmail.com